ISBN 978-0-331-47401-5
PIBN 10271150

English
Français
Deutsche
Italiano
Español
Português

www.forgottenbooks.com

Mythology Photography **Fiction**
Fishing Christianity **Art** Cooking
Essays Buddhism Freemasonry
Medicine **Biology** Music **Ancient
Egypt** Evolution Carpentry Physics
Dance Geology **Mathematics** Fitness
Shakespeare **Folklore** Yoga Marketing
Confidence Immortality Biographies
Poetry **Psychology** Witchcraft
Electronics Chemistry History **Law**
Accounting **Philosophy** Anthropology
Alchemy Drama Quantum Mechanics
Atheism Sexual Health **Ancient History**
Entrepreneurship Languages Sport
Paleontology Needlework Islam
Metaphysics Investment Archaeology
Parenting Statistics Criminology
Motivational

ORDINANCES

PROMULGATED BY THE

GOVERNOR GENERAL OF THE SUDAN

TOGETHER WITH

SELECTED PROCLAMATIONS NOTICES RULES AND

ORDERS ISSUED WITH REFERENCE THERETO

IN THE YEARS 1899 TO 1905.

Printed and published

by the Authority of the Governor General.

CAIRO:

AL-MOKATTAM PRINTING OFFICE

1907.

Anglo Egyptian Sudan: Statutes.

PREFACE.

This collection of the Sudan Ordinances and Selected Proclamations Notices Rules and Orders, is a reprint from the Sudan Gazettes, with slight clerical amendments, of the Ordinances. of the Sudan Government from the first constitution of the Government down to the end of the year 1905 together with some of the more important Proclamations Notices Rules and Orders published in the Sudan Gazette for the same period.

The Ordinances are arranged in chronological order and immediately following each Ordinance are the Proclamations Notices Rules and Orders which relate to it.

Where an Ordinance has been amended reference is made to the amending Ordinance which will be found in its proper place.

The title only of repealed Ordinances is given with notes stating in what Gazettes they were published and how they were repealed.

This reprint is published pursuant to the Revision Ordinance 1906 and may be used as the authorised English version of the Ordinances contained therein.

The Ordinances are printed as amended by the Revision Ordinance 1906 and the Revision Ordinance (No. 2) 1906 and the opportunity has also been taken to correct several clerical errors which were found in the Gazettes.

The Sudan Penal Code, the Code of Criminal Procedure and the Civil Justice Ordinance 1900 which were printed separately are not included in this volume.

This reprint has been edited in the Legal Secretary's Office.

TABLE OF CONTENTS.

APPENDIX.

ADDENDUM.

The Revision Ordinance (No. 2.) 1906 referred to on pages 70, 71, 77, 141, 142, 147, 148, 156 and 158 is numbered "1906 No. 6." and was published in Sudan Gazette No. 106 of 1 February 1907.

1899 No. 1.

THE KHARTOUM, BERBER AND DONGOLA TOWN LANDS ORDINANCE 1899.

Promulgated in the Sudan Gazette, No. 2, of 27 May, 1899. Re-promulgated with alterations in Sudan Gazette, No. 4, of 9 September, 1899. Printed as re-promulgated.

Amended by the Khartoum, Berber and Dongola Town Lands Ordinance, 1901 (Sud. Gaz., No. 19, of 1 January, 1901) 1901 No. 1, and by the Kassala and Kordofan Town Lands Ordinance, 1904 (Sud. Gaz., No. 59, February, 1904). 1904 No. 2.

An Ordinance for settling questions as to lands situate within the towns of Khartoum, Berber and Dongola, and for providing for the laying out and rebuilding of the said towns.

WHEREAS, during the recent rebellion, the towns of Khartoum, Berber and Dongola have been reduced to ruins, and the lands and buildings therein contained have been abandoned, and the names of the former proprietors are in many cases unknown, as also whether they are alive or dead, and who are the representatives of such as are dead ;

And whereas it is expedient that the said towns should be laid out anew and rebuilt, in such manner as to make proper provision for the health and convenience of the inhabitants;

And whereas a Commission has already been appointed to receive and consider all claims in respect of lands situate within the town of Khartoum.

IT IS HEREBY ENACTED as follows :

1. The towns of Khartoum, Berber and Dongola respectively, shall, for the purposes of this Ordinance, include the whole of the respective areas enclosed within the lines of the old fortifications and the river. *Limits of town areas.*

2. The Commission already appointed for Khartoum shall be reconstituted so as to consist of three commissioned officers of the Egyptian Army (whether engaged in military or civil work) and two Notables of the locality ; and as so reconstituted is continued as a Commission, with the title of the Khartoum Town Lands Commission, for the purposes of this Ordinance. *Constitution of Commission.*

Berber and
Dongola
Commissions.

3. Commissions similarly constituted, with the respective titles of the Berber Town Lands Commission and the Dongola Town Lands Commission, shall be appointed for Berber and Dongola, respectively.

Presentation of
claims.

4. Every person claiming to be entitled to the ownership of lands or of any share in lands, in any of the towns of Khartoum, Berber, or Dongola, shall present his claim to the Commission for that town not later than the 31st day of December, 1899, under penalty of forfeiture. A claim may be presented to a Commission either by writing addressed to the President of the Commission and deposited at, or sent by registered letter to the Mudiria or other prescribed place, or personally or by a duly accredited agent, at any public sitting of the Commission. Claims already presented to the Khartoum Commission need not be re-presented.

Contents of
claims.

5. Every claim shall describe the land in respect of which it is made, sufficiently for its identification, and shall state its area, and whether it is, or was, building land, or garden land, or under cultivation, and whether the entirety of the land is claimed, or an undivided share only, and shall indicate the nature of the title under which the claim is made.

List of claims.

6. Each Commission shall keep a list of claims presented to it and the absence of any claim from the list shall be *prima facie* evidence that the claim has not been presented.

Adjudication
on claims.

7. Each Commission shall adjudicate upon the claims presented to it, after giving such reasonable notice as shall be possible to the claimants, and after hearing them, or their duly accredited agents, if they present themselves. The Commission shall then enter opposite to each claim, upon the list of claims, a statement as to whether it is admitted wholly, or to any and what extent, or whether it is rejected. The decision of the Commission upon any claim shall be final, unless the Governor General shall, upon the petition of the claimant to be presented within 30 days after adjudication, order that the case be reheard.

Garden land or
land under
cultivation.

8. All land which is now garden land or under cultivation, and every share therein, a claim to which is admitted, may be purchased by the Government by payment of the fair price, which shall be fixed by the Commission. In fixing the price the Commission shall make no allowance for the purposes for which the Government

intends to employ the land, nor for anything already done thereon by the Government.

9. In place of every piece of land other than garden land or land under cultivation, to which a claim shall be admitted, there shall be allotted to the claimant a piece of land in the town, of equal or greater area, and, upon such allotment being made, the title of the claimant to the original piece of the land, and all his interest therein, shall absolutely determine. In fixing the land to be allotted to the claimant, regard shall be had, so far as possible, to the purpose for which he intends to use the land, which purpose he shall be bound to state to the Commission.

Allotment of land other than garden land or land under cultivation.

10. Every allotment shall impose upon the allottee the obligation to erect upon the land allotted, within two years from the earliest date at which allotments shall be made, or one year from the date of the particular allotment, whichever period shall be the longer, a building conforming to the Tanzim regulations hereafter to be issued.

Allottee to erect building.

§ *10 Amended by the Khurtoum, Berber and Dongola Town Lands Ordinance, 1901 (Sud. Gaz., No. 19). 1901 No. 1.*

11. Where a claim is admitted to an undivided share in land, it shall be sufficient to allot to the claimant a piece of land bearing to the whole area of the original plot the proportion which his admitted share in the original plot bears to its entirety.

Land held in undivided shares.

12. Where the allotment to which a claimant is entitled is less than the minimum area on which, under the Tanzim regulations to be issued, a dwelling house may be erected, such minimum area may be allotted, or the Government may purchase the share of the claimant at a fair price, to be fixed in manner aforesaid.

Allotment of area too small for dwelling house.

13. Claims in respect of date palms and other fruit-bearing trees shall be made, and such trees may be purchased by the Government, in accordance with the provisions hereinbefore contained as to claims in respect of, and purchase of, garden lands, so far as the same are applicable.

Date palms and other fruit bearing trees.

14. No sale, or transfer *inter vivos*, of a claim to land, nor any charge thereon, shall have any validity. No sale, or transfer *inter vivos*, of an allotment before it has been built upon in accordance with Section 10 shall have any validity, unless and until it shall

Transfer of claims and allotments.

be registered in the land register together with an undertaking by the purchaser, or transferee, to build thereon in accordance with the provisions of, and within the time specified by, Section 10.

Forfeited lands and trees.

15. All lands and trees in the said towns, other than lands allotted under Section 9 or garden or cultivated lands or trees to which a claim is admitted but which are not purchased by the Government under the provisions of Section 8 or Section 13, as also all lands allotted but not built on in accordance with the provisions of, and within the time specified by Section 10, shall become and be the absolute property of the Government.

Claims against the Government.

16. No person shall have any claim or right of action whatsoever against the Government in respect of any lands or trees in any of the said towns, or in respect of anything to be done under this Ordinance, save in accordance with the provisions of this Ordinance.

Interpretation.

17. In this Ordinance the masculine shall include the feminine, words importing the singular shall include the plural, and words importing an individual shall include a body corporate.

Short title.

18. This Ordinance may be cited as the Khartoum, Berber and Dongola Town Lands Ordinance, 1899.

In connection with the above Ordinance, the following Proclamations have been made :—

A.

Promulgated in the Sudan Gazette No. 42, of December 1902.
Amended by Proclamations of May 1 1903, Sud. Gaz. No. 47, and July 1 1904, Sud. Gaz. No. 64, Proclamations B and C infra.

KHARTOUM TOWN LANDS ORDINANCE.
Proclamation.

WHEREAS by the Khartoum, Berber and Dongola Town Lands Ordinance 1899, after reciting that the said towns had been reduced to ruins and that it was expedient that they should be laid out anew and rebuilt in such manner as to make proper provision for the health and convenience of the inhabitants and after constituting Commissions for adjudicating upon all claims to the ownership of lands or of any share of land in the said towns and after providing that in place of every piece of land other than garden land or land under cultivation to which a claim should be admitted there should be allotted to the claimant a piece of land in the town of equal or greater area, it was enacted as follows :—

Section 10.—Every allotment shall impose upon the allottee the obligation to erect upon the land allotted within two years from the earliest date at which such allotments shall be made or one year from the date of the particular allotment whichever period shall be the longer, a building according to the Tanzim Regulations hereafter to be issued. And by Section 15 of the same Ordinance it was enacted amongst other matters that all lands allotted but not built on in accordance with the provisions of and within the time specified by Section 10 should become and be the absolute property of the Government. And whereas by the Khartoum, Berber and Dongola Town Lands Ordinance 1901, the time within which under Section 10 of the recited Ordinance of 1899, an allottee of land was under obligation to erect a building on the land allotted to him was extended as follows :—

1901 No. 1.

If the allotment was made or notice that the Commission was ready to fix the allotment was given on or before the 31st December, 1900, the time was extended to the 31st December, 1902, if notice that the Commission was ready to fix the allotment was given for the first time after the 31st December, 1900, the time was extended to two years from the date of such notice.

And whereas there are a considerable number of allotments in the town of Khartoum which have not yet been built on in accordance with Section 10 of the recited Ordinance of 1899, and the extended time within which the same are required to be built on will in most cases expire on 31st day of December next.

Now it is hereby declared as follows :—

1. By virtue of Section 15 of the recited Ordinance of 1899, all lands in the town of Khartoum allotted but not built on in accordance with the provisions of and within the time specified by the recited Ordinance of 1899, as varied by the recited Ordinance of 1901, shall become and be the absolute property of Government.

Lands allotted but not built upon to be forfeited.

1899 No. 1.

1901 No. 1.

Lists of lands.

2. Lists of lands which the Government claims to have become thus forfeited, will be published by the Mudir from time to time. and unless the forfeited owners show good reasons to the contrary, applications will, if necessary, be made to the courts to give effect to the said forfeitures.

Re-sale.

3. The Controller, Sudan Government, is authorised to receive applications for the purchase of any forfeited land subject to the condition that the purchaser will at once commence and within nine months of the date of the sale complete a building upon the said land in accordance with the Tanzim Regulations. Any land in respect of which such an application is received will be put up for sale by auction or tender subject to a reserve price.

Application should now be made to the Governor of the Province. v. Proclamation of May. 1, 1903. Sud. Gaz. No. 47. Proclamation B infra.

Privileges granted.

4. As a matter of grace the Governor General will grant to the owners of lands allotted under the recited Ordinances which become forfeitable previously to the 31st December, 1903, the privileges mentioned hereafter.

(1) In the case of lands held at the time of forfeiture by the original allottees thereof.

By an original allottee is meant a person who received his allotment in lieu of land which belonged to him previously to the publication of the Khartoum, Berber and Dongola Town Lands Ordinance, 1899, it does not include a person who received his allotment in lieu of claims purchased after that date.

1899 No. 1.

(*a*) In the event of the Government selling an allotment the amount of the purchase money less 5 per cent thereof to cover the costs of the sale will be returned to the late owner.

(*b*) If the late owner of an allotment which has not yet been sold nor is about to be put up for sale notifies to the Controller his desire to build upon the said allotment and produces guarantees to the satisfaction of the Controller that he will at once begin the building and complete the same within nine months in accordance with the Tanzim Regulations he will be permitted without payment to re-enter upon the said allotment and erect the said building and in the event of the said building being completed within the time and in the manner aforesaid the Governor General will re-grant the said allotment to him.

(2) In case of lands held at the time of forfeiture by owners who have acquired the same by purchase.

(a) In the event of the Government selling an allotment within two years of its having become liable to forfeiture the following proportion of the sale money will be returned to the late owners namely 90 per cent if the sale takes place the first year, 80 per cent if the sale takes place in the second year.

(b) If within the said period of two years the late owner of an allotment which has not yet been sold nor is about to be put up for sale notifies to the Controller his desire to build upon the said land and produces guarantees to the satisfaction of the Controller that he will at once begin building and complete the same within nine months in accordance with the Tanzim Regulations he will be permitted upon payment of a fine to be fixed by the Controller equivalent to 10 per cent of the value of the land if such building is begun the first year and to 20 per cent of the value of the land if such building is begun in the second year to enter upon the allotment and erect the said building and in the event of the said building being completed within the time and in the manner aforesaid, the Governor General will re-grant the said allotment to him.

§ 4 *amended by Proclamation of May 1, 1903. Sud. Gaz. No. 47. Proclamation B infra.*

5. The said privileges will continue grantable in respect of lands held at the time of forfeiture by the original allottees thereof until the Governor General withdraws the same but in respect of land held at the time of forfeiture by owners who have acquired the same by purchase they will be grantable for a period of two years only from the time when such lands become forfeitable and will then entirely cease. They shall not be suable for at law. *How long such privileges grantable.*

§ 5 *amended by Proclamation of July, 1904. Sud. Gaz. No. 64. Proclamation C infra.*

6. The Governor General reserves the right at any time to revoke or vary the terms of this Proclamation. *Reservation.*

B.

Promulgated in the Sudan Gazette No. 47 of May 1st 1903.

KHARTOUM TOWN LANDS ORDINANCE.

WITH reference to the Proclamation under the above title published in the Sudan Gazette No. 42 it is hereby declared :—

1—that applications with reference to forfeited land should be made to the Mudir of Khartoum and not to the Controller

2—that all duties in connection therewith directed to be performed by the Controller shall be performed by the Mudir of Khartoum

3—that forfeited land may be sold by the Government by private contract if the late owners express their consent to the sale

and the said Proclamation is hereby amended accordingly.

C.

Promulgated in the Sudan Gazette No. 64 of July 1st 1904.
Explained by Proclamation of September 1 1905. Sud. Gaz. No. 81, Proclamation D infra.

KHARTOUM TOWN LANDS ORDINANCE.

Proclamation.

WITH reference to the Proclamation of December 1902 under the Khartoum Town Lands Ordinance published in Sudan Gazette No. 42 page 70, it is hereby proclaimed as follows :—

In case of the sales of lands held at the time of forfeiture by owners who have acquired the same by purchase, the period within which 90 per cent of the sale money will be returned to the late owner, and within which he is permitted to re-enter upon the land for the purpose of building subject to a fine equivalent to 10 per cent of the value of the land, as provided in Section 4 Subsection 2 of the said Proclamation, is extended until further order, and will not be withdrawn except after at least one year's notice.

Upon the sale of forfeited land the Governor with the approval of the Director of Lands, will fix as reserve price a sum not less than the average market price of similar land, unless the late owner requests that the land shall be sold without reserve.

The time within which buildings on forfeited land must be completed is extended from nine months to one year from the date of sale or from the date of the late owner notifying his desire to re-enter and build, as the case may be.

D.

Promulgated in the Sudan Gazette No. 81 of September 1st 1905.

KHARTOUM TOWN LANDS ORDINANCE.

WHEREAS it has been reported to the Government that the Proclamation contained in Sudan Gazette No. 64 page 226 of July 1st 1904 has been commonly interpreted to mean that until further order, which will not take effect for one year after notice thereof, owners who have acquired by purchase forfeited lands are discharged from any obligation to build on the said land by paying ten per cent of the value thereof at the expiration of every year. *Proclamation C supra.*

Notice is hereby given that such an interpretation is a mistaken one and that under Clause 4 Sub-Section 2 (*b*) of the Proclamation of December 1902 as modified by the said Proclamation of July 1st 1904 the right to a re-grant from the Governor General is lost on the first failure to carry out the building within the period of one year according to the guarantee and that the guarantors on this default are liable to be called upon to pay the amount of their guarantee. *Proclamation A supra. Proclamation C supra.*

To avoid all questions notice is also given that all land which has been bought from Government and conveyed to the purchaser under the usual form of Land Certificate is bound strictly by the conditions in such certificate.

1899 No. 2.

THE TITLE OF LANDS ORDINANCE, 1899.

Promulgated in the Sud. Gaz. No. 2. of 27 May, 1899.
Amended by the Title of Lands Ordinance, 1903. (Sud. Gaz. No. 45, of March, 1903). 1903 No. 3. See Note "a."

An Ordinance for settling disputes as to land and for the registration of titles.

WHEREAS by Khedivial Decree of the 1st day of April, 1897, provision has been made for the settlement of disputes as to the ownership of land in the Province of Dongola, and it is expedient to make similar provision for other parts of the Sudan :

And whereas the preparation of registers of title in connection therewith provides a basis for improvement in the system of land registration.

IT IS HEREBY ENACTED as follows :—

DISPUTED TITLES TO LAND.

Appointment of Commission.

1. *A Commission, consisting of three Commissioned Officers in the Egyptian Army (whether engaged in military or civil work) and two notables of the Province, shall be appointed in each of the Provinces of Khartoum and Berber, and in such other provinces, districts, and towns, as the Governor General may, from time to time, determine by notice published in the "Sudan Gazette," to receive and adjudicate upon claims to land.*

Preamble and § 1 repealed by Title of Lands Ordinance, 1903 (Sud. Gaz., No. 45) 1903 No. 3.

Claims to land not in possession of claimant or to mortgages.

2. Every person claiming to be entitled to land of which he is not in possession, or, to any mortgage or charge upon land or upon the produce of land in a province, district or town for which a Commission shall be appointed otherwise than land in the towns of Khartoum and Berber, shall present his claim to the Commission, in writing, at the Mudiria or other appointed place, not later than the 31st day of December, 1899, or such later date as may be specified *in the Order appointing the Commission,* under penalty of forfeiture.

§ 2. Words in italics rep. by Title of Lands Ordinance 1903 (Sud. Gaz. No. 45). 1903 No. 3.

3. The Commission shall adjudicate upon the claim, after giving such reasonable notice to the claimant and to the person in possession, if any, as shall be possible, and after hearing them, or their duly authorised agents, if they present themselves, and, save as against a person subsequently claiming within the time allowed by law, the decision of the commission shall be final.

Adjudication upon claims.

§ *3 added to by Title of Lands Ordinance 1903 (Sud. Gaz. No. 45). 1903 No. 3.*

4. The Commission shall prepare a register upon which there shall be entered the particulars of all land in respect of which a claim is established, and shall inscribe therein, as owner, the name of every claimant who is admitted to be the owner of land, whether absolutely, or subject to charges, and particulars of the interest of every claimant who is admitted to have an interest therein less than that of an owner.

Register of land when claim established.

5. Where the right of a claimant is admitted in respect only of an undivided share in land, and no claim to the remaining share in the land is made within the time allowed by law, or such claim, if made, is rejected, the claimant shall be entitled to the entirety of the land. Nevertheless, in such case, the persons entitled to the remaining share in the land shall be allowed a further period of one year from the last day for making claims, in which to come in and claim their rights.

Procedure when claims to undivided shares established.

6. In adjudicating upon claims the following rules shall apply :—

Rules of adjudication.

I. Where it is shewn that a person has been in possession of land, or in receipt of the rents or profits thereof, at each of two periods, it shall be presumed that he has been in continuous possession of the land, or in continuous receipt of the rents or profits, between those periods, until the contrary be shewn, and no account shall be taken of interruption of possession, or of the receipt of rents or profits, owing to *force majeure* :

II. Continuous possession, or receipt of rents or profits, during the five years immediately preceding the date of claim, shall create an absolute title as against all persons :

III. Every person claiming land of which he is not in possession and of the rents and profits of which he is not in receipt, shall be required to prove that he was formerly in possession, or in actual receipt of the rents or profits, with a good title, and that such possession, or receipt of rents or profits, was, during the recent rebellion, terminated by *force majeure :*

IV. In default of any claimant with a superior title, continuous possession since the re-establishment of the civil authority shall create a *prima facie* title :

V. Possession or receipt of rents or profits, by any person through whom a claimant derives his title, shall be deemed to have been the possession, or receipt of rents or profits, of the claimant :

VI. Where, from the relationship of the parties or from other special cause, it appears that the possessor of land is, or was, in possession on behalf of another, his possession shall be deemed to be, or to have been, the possession of that other.

Minors and unborn persons.

7. Where it appears to the Commission in the course of its enquiry, that a claim might be established by a minor, or by an unborn person if born, a person shall be appointed to represent the minor or unborn person, and the minor, or unborn person shall be deemed to have made a claim within the time allowed by law.

Procedure when persons entitled do not claim.

8. If the Commission be satisfied that any person who has not presented a claim is entitled to any land, or to a mortgage or charge upon any land or the produce thereof, the Commission may, but shall not be bound to, proceed as if he had made a claim within the time allowed by law.

Claimants dispossessed during the rebellion.

9. Where a claimant proves that he was formerly in possession of land with a good title but was dispossessed thereof by *force majeure* during the rebellion, and some other person is now entitled to the land under the foregoing rules, the Commission shall report the case to the Governor General who shall, so far as possible, make to such claimants grants of land of equal area and in as favourable situation. Such grants may be made subject to any conditions as to occupation and cultivation, and the decision of the Governor General on all questions which arise shall be final.

Application of Ordinance.

10. No right to any interest in land which might have been made the subject of a claim under this Ordinance, shall be enforceable otherwise than in accordance with the provisions of this Ordinance.

Registration of Land.

11. Whenever a land register shall have been established for any province, district, or town, no evidence shall be receivable in any Civil Court (otherwise than in an action, or other proceeding, for the rectification of the register) :   *Effect of registration of land.*

   I. Of the sale, or other transfer *inter vivos*, of land within the province, district, or town unless and until the name of the purchaser, or transferee, shall have been inscribed in the register as owner of the land :

   II. Of a mortgage or charge of or upon the land or the produce thereof, unless the mortgage or charge is created by an instrument in writing, and the instrument or notice thereof has been inscribed in the register :

   III. Of a sale or other transfer *inter vivos* of a registered mortgage or charge, unless and until the name of the purchaser or transferee has been inscribed on the register as entitled to the benefit of the mortgage or charge.

12. Every entry on a land register shall be *prima facie* evidence of the facts therein stated.   *Entry in register to be prima facie evidence.*

13. A registered dealing with land for value made without notice of a prior unregistered dealing shall have priority over such unregistered dealing even although it be subsequently registered.   *Priority as between registered and unregistered dealings with land.*

14. The above provisions as to registration shall not affect the right to acquire a title to land by prescription.   *Prescription.*

Definitions etc.

15. In this Ordinance, unless the context otherwise requires, the singular shall include the plural; the masculine shall include the feminine; "claimant" shall include a person in possession, although he does not make a formal claim; and "land" shall include (i) an undivided share in land, (ii) the right to cultivate a determinate or determinable area of land, although its situation may vary from year to year, and (iii) trees.   *Interpretation.*

Short title. **16.** This Ordinance may be cited as the Title of Lands Ordinance, 1899.

(a) The Title of Lands Ordinance 1903 (1903 No. 3.) repealed the preamble and § 1 of the Ordinance of 1899, and substituted for § 1 the following :

"A Land Commission shall be appointed in such provinces, districts, and towns as the Governor General may from time to time determine by notice published in the Sudan Gazette, to receive and adjudicate upon claims to land. Such Commission shall consist of five members selected by the Governor General of whom not less than two shall be natives of the Sudan."

For the words "in the Order appointing the Commission" in § 2 of the Ordinance of 1899, the words "by notice published in the Sudan Gazette" were substituted by the Ordinance of 1903.

The Ordinance of 1903 empowered the Commission to rehear cases upon petition presented within six months.

With reference to the above Ordinance the following Proclamations have been made.

A.

Promulgated in the Sudan Gazette No. 10 of 1 April 1900.

PROCLAMATION.

WHEREAS it has been brought to the notice of His Excellency the Governor General of the Sudan that certain persons taking advantage of the want of money in the Sudan are acquiring lands from the inhabitants at prices below the actual value, notice is hereby given that until such time as it may be found possible to establish a Land Register as contemplated by Sec. 11 of the Title of Lands Ordinance 1899, all contracts for the purchase of lands should be submitted to the Mudir for approval and that power will be given to Land Commissions which may be appointed under the provisions of the said Ordinance to revise the terms of any sales

1899 No. 2.

which may be proved to have taken place under the circumstances aforesaid and of which notice shall not have been given to the Mudir.

B.

Promulgated in the Sudan Gazette No. 78 of 1 July 1905.

PROCLAMATION.

WHEREAS it is desired to take further measures to prevent the disposal of lands by natives of the Sudan before their rights to the same have been settled, and also to prevent them from being induced to dispose of the same at inadequate prices.

It is hereby proclaimed and ordered as follows:—

1. No native of the Sudan may sell mortgage charge or otherwise dispose of nor agree to sell mortgage charge or dispose of any land or any right or interest in or over the same unless with the written consent of the Governor of the Province within which such land is situated—provided, however, that such consent shall not be required to a devise by will or lease for a period not exceeding three years.

2. Every sale mortgage charge or other disposition by a native of the Sudan of any land or any right or interest in or over the same and every agreement for the sale mortgage charge or other disposition of the same (except a devise by will or lease for a period not exceeding three years) to which the consent in writing of the Governor has not been expressed, shall be null and void.

3. Money paid after the publication of this Proclamation to any native of the Sudan in consideration of any sale mortgage charge or other disposition as aforesaid or of any agreement for the same (except a lease for a period not exceeding three years) to which the consent in writing of the Governor has not been expressed, shall not be recoverable nor suable for.

1899 No. 3.

THE LAND TAX ORDINANCE 1899.

Promulgated in the Sudan Gazette No. 2, of 27 May 1899. Re-promulgated with alterations in Sudan Gazette No. 4 of 9 September 1899.   Printed as re-promulgated. Amended by the Land Tax Ordinance 1901. (Sud. Gaz. No. 26 of 1 August 1901) 1901 No. 6, and by the Land Tax Ordinance 1905 (Sud. Gaz. No. 82 of 1 October 1905) 1905 No. 11.

An Ordinance for regulating the Land Tax and Date Tax.

IT IS HEREBY ENACTED as follows :—

Rates at which land tax to be levied.

1. Land tax on lands other than land dependent on the rainfall (Dahari) shall be levied in such provinces and districts as the Governor General shall, from time to time, order by notice in the "Sudan Gazette" at the rates following, that is to say :—

(a) *Island land irrigable by means of sakias or shadoofs :*
   1st class lands 60 P.T. per feddan.
   2nd class lands 50 P.T. per feddan.

(b) *Land on the mainland irrigable by means of sakias or shadoofs:*
   1st class lands 40 P.T. per feddan.
   2nd class lands 30 P.T. per feddan.

(c) *Foreshore land irrigable by flood :*
   (Selooka) 20 P.T. per feddan.

(d) *Land irrigable from wells :*
   (Matara) 20 P.T. per feddan.

§ *1. Words in Italics in § 1 repealed by the Land Tax Ordinance 1901, (Sud. Gaz. No. 26) 1901 No. 6 which was repealed by the Land Tax Ordinance 1905 (Sud. Gaz. No. 82 of 1 October 1905) 1905 No.11. The Ordinance of 1905 imposed the following rates in place of those specified in § 1 of the Ordinance of 1899:*

1st	rate	...	...	P.T. 60 per feddan.
2nd	rate	...	...	P.T. 50 per feddan.
3rd	rate	...	...	P.T. 40 per feddan.
4th	rate	...	...	P.T. 30 per feddan.
5th	rate	...	...	P.T. 20 per feddan.
6th	rate	...	...	P.T. 10 per feddan.

Tax on date trees.

2. The tax on date trees in such provinces and districts as the Governor General shall order in manner aforesaid, shall be levied at the rate of P.T. 2 on every tree, whether male or female, which has commenced to bear. Provided that there shall be exempt from taxation all trees growing in the court or garden of a house assessed for house tax, when the value of such court or garden is taken account of in estimating the annual rental value of the house.

3. The Mudir shall issue regulations for the classification of lands and for the assessment of the above mentioned taxes; and shall fix, and give sufficient public notice of, the instalments by which, and the times at which, the taxes shall be paid. In fixing the amount of the instalments and the dates for payment the Mudir shall have regard to the times at which the various crops are gathered. *Regulations to be issued by the Mudir.*

4. Whenever any part of the land tax is more than one calendar month in arrear, the prescribed official shall report the case to the Inspector or the Mudir, who shall issue a summons addressed to the owner or owners of the land by name, or as such owner or owners, directing his or their appearance before him. Such summons may be served on any one of the owners (if more than one) on behalf of the rest. If none of the owners is resident in the village, or none of them is known or can, after the exercise of due diligence, be found, the summons may be served in any manner authorised by law or by fixing it in a prominent place in the village. *When land tax in arrear, summons to be served on owner.*

5. If upon the hearing of the summons, the Magistrate is satisfied that the crop upon the land has failed through no fault of the owner or cultivator, and that the tax cannot be paid without depriving the owner of the means of earning his living as an agriculturalist, the Magistrate may adjourn the summons and report the case to the Mudir for reference to the Governor General. *Case in which summons may be adjourned.*

6. Subject to the provisions of the preceding section, the Magistrate shall issue a warrant for the attachment of the land, in manner hereinafter prescribed, and shall pass an order directing the Mamur to issue process for the recovery of the whole sum then in arrear in respect of land tax. *Warrant for attachment of land and order for recovery of sum in arrear.*

7. In order to recover the sum due, the Mamur shall first issue a warrant for the seizure of any money or other movable property of the owner or owners in default or of any of them. *Seizure of movable property.*

Provided that there shall be exempt from seizure under this section :

(1) The necessary clothing of an owner, his wife or children :
(2) The tools of an artizan, or the implements of a cultivator :
(3) Cattle ordinarily employed by their owner in agriculture and necessary in the opinion of the Magistrate to his continuing to earn his livelihood by agriculture.

Ascertainment of movable property.

8. For the purpose of ascertaining the movable property of the owner or owners, any person may be summoned by the Magistrate or Mamur to appear before him and may be examined.

Sale of goods.

9. If the sum in arrear be not paid within 14 days of seizure under Section 7, the goods seized, or a part thereof sufficient to meet the arrears of the tax and the costs of the proceedings, shall be sold by the Mamur by public auction.   Provided that goods of a perishable nature may be sold at once.

Sale of crop.

10. If the sum raised under the preceding section be insufficient to meet the arrears of the tax and the costs of the proceedings, or no such sum can, with due diligence, be raised, and there is a growing crop upon the land, the Mamur shall so soon as the crop is ripe issue a warrant for the seizure of the crop, and for the immediate sale of the crop, or a competent part thereof, by public auction.

Sale of cattle.

11. If there be no crop, or if the proceeds of sale of the crop when sold are insufficient, the Mamur shall issue a warrant for the seizure and immediate sale in manner aforesaid of the cattle exempted from seizure under Clause (3) of the proviso to Section 7.

Sale of land.

12. If, after the steps described in the preceding sections have been taken, there is still any part of the tax in arrear, the Mamur shall sell the land or a competent part thereof by public auction.

Provided that the land shall in no case be sold until a period of 2 calendar months at the least has elapsed since the commencement of proceedings.

A sale of land under this Section shall confer on the purchaser a title to the land free from all incumbrances.

Proceeds of sale.

13. The proceeds of sale under this Ordinance shall be applied in the first instance in satisfaction of the costs in the proceedings,

and next in payment of arrears of tax; and the balance shall be remitted to the magistrate for payment to the persons appearing to be entitled thereto.

14. Where there is a *bona fide* question as to the ownership of any property seized or attached under this Ordinance or as to the persons entitled to the balance of the proceeds of sale, the Mamur may stay proceedings, and try the question if it be within his competence, or refer it for trial to the Magistrate. *(Question as to ownership of property seized or of proceeds of sale.)*

15. If upon the hearing of the summons mentioned in Section 4, the Magistrate is satisfied that the owner has not, or that the owners have not, wilfully neglected to pay, or attempted to escape payment of the tax, and that there is a growing crop upon the land, he may issue a warrant for the attachment of the land and pass an order directing the Mamur to proceed against the crop when ripe under Section 10 before proceeding under Section 7. *(When neglect to pay not wilful, growing crop may be seized.)*

16. If it be made to appear to the Magistrate at any stage of the proceedings that the cultivation of the growing crop mentioned in Section 10 or Section 15 is being neglected, he shall pass an order directing the Mamur to proceed as if there were no growing crop. *(Saving when growing crop is being neglected.)*

17. Attachment of land shall be effected by proclamation in the village and by giving notice to the Omdeh or Sheikh of the village. *(Method and effect of attaching land.)*

It shall operate to render invalid any sale or transfer of, or charge upon, the land or the produce thereof or of or upon the cattle or implements of agriculture employed in the cultivation thereof, which shall be made, without the consent of the Magistrate, prior to the removal of the attachment.

18. When any part of the date tax is more than one calendar month in arrear, payment may be enforced against the owners and against all date trees owned by them, in the same manner, so far as may be, as payment of land tax is enforced against land and its owners. *(Date tax in arrear.)*

19. Co-owners of land or date trees in undivided shares shall be jointly and severally liable for land or date tax. *(Co-owners.)*

Interpretation.

20. In this Ordinance " the Magistrate " shall mean the Mudir or Inspector by whom the original summons is issued, or his successor in office.

Short title. .

21. This Ordinance may be cited as the Land Tax Ordinance, 1899.

In connection with this Ordinance the following notices have been published.

A.

A series of notices published in Sudan Gazette No. 6 of November 2, 1899; No. 8 of January 2, 1900; No. 18 of November 1, 1900; No. 19 of January 1, 1901; No. 22 of April 1, 1901; No. 31 of January 31, 1902; and No. 43 of January 1903 whereby the Governor General ordered that this Ordinance should have effect in the provinces and districts therein respectively mentioned.

These have been cancelled by the notice C infra.

B.

Published in " Sudan Gazette" No. 46 of April 1903.

In order to encourage the erection of sakias notice is hereby given that for the first year after the erection of a new sakia the land irrigated by such sakia will be exempt from land tax provided that land tax was not during the previous year charged on such land.

By a later notice, published in "Sudan Gazette" No. 48, of 1 June 1903, the words "new sakia" were explained to mean "a sakia in addition to sakias already existing and not a sakia erected in substitution for an already existing sakia."

C.

Published in Sudan Gazette No. 86 of January 1, 1906.

LAND TAX AND DATE TAX.

1899 No. 3.

All previous notices made under sections 1 and 2 of the Land Tax Ordinance 1899 whereby the Governor General ordered that the said Ordinance should take effect in various provinces and districts are hereby cancelled and in lieu thereof the Governor General in exercise of the powers conferred upon him by sections 1 and 2 of the Land Tax Ordinance 1899 hereby orders that the *1899 No. 3.* said Ordinance shall take effect in the following Provinces and Districts that is to say:—

In the Provinces of Halfa, Dongola, Berber, Khartoum and Kassala; and

In the Markazes of Geteina and Kawa in the White Nile Province;

The Markaz of Tokar in the Red Sea Province;

The Markazes of Kamlin, Rufaa, Messalamia, Wad Medani and Wad Medani Town in the Blue Nile Province;

The Markaz of Sennar in the Province of Sennar;

And the Markaz of Bara in the Province of Kordofan.

As regards lands recently brought into cultivation or as yet uncultivated, which are liable to land tax, the said Ordinance shall take effect subject to such exemptions as have been approved by the Governor General and published in Province Orders or shall hereafter be approved and published in like manner.

Governors of Provinces will pursuant to section 3 of the said Ordinance from time to time classify the lands (other than land dependent on the rainfall which will remain subject to the collection of ushur as heretofore) within the said Provinces and Districts for the purpose of land tax; land tax will not be collected on lands omitted from such classification.

1899 No. 4.

THE ROYALTIES ON GUM ETC. ORDINANCE 1899.

Promulgated in Sud. Gaz. No. 2 of 27 May 1899.
Repealed by the Royalties on Gum etc. Ordinance 1904 (Sud. Gaz. No. 66 of 7 September 1904). 1904 No. 7.

1899 No. 5.

THE ARMS ORDINANCE 1899.

Promulgated in Sud. Gaz. No. 2 of 27 May 1899.
Repealed by the Arms Ordinance 1903. (Sud. Gaz. No. 49 of 1 July 1903). 1903 No. 8.

1899 No. 6.

THE LICENCE (LIQUOR) ORDINANCE 1899.

Promulgated in Sud. Gaz. No. 3 of 27 May 1899.

An Ordinance for regulating and licensing the sale of Alcoholic Liquors.

IT IS HEREBY ENACTED as follows :—

Licence necessary for persons importing wines etc. into the Sudan.

Penalties.

1. No person or company shall import into the Sudan, trade in, or sell, any wines, spirits, or other alcoholic liquors, except in virtue of a licence to be issued by the Mudir, after inquiry as to the character of the applicant, under penalty of a fine not exceeding L.E. 100 and confiscation of all wines spirits or other alcoholic liquors in the possession or ownership, or upon the premises of the offender. The licence shall specify the premises upon which the business is to be carried on.

Fee for licence.

2. The fee for a licence shall be L.E. 50, payable by equal half-yearly instalments on the 1st day of January and the 1st day of July in each year. Whenever a licence is taken out otherwise than at the beginning of a year, the instalment for the current half year shall be paid at the time of obtaining the licence.

Duration of licence.

3. Every licence shall expire on the 31st day of December in each year, but no penalty shall be incurred if the licence is renewed on or before the 14th day of January then next ensuing.

Revocation of licence.

4. The holders of licences shall conform to regulations to be issued as to the conduct of their business, under penalty of revocation of the licence, and of any other penalties which may be specified in the regulations. But no revocation of a licence shall be effective unless passed or confirmed by the Mudir.

Sale carried on at more than one place.

5. Any person or company desiring to carry on at more places than one, (and in conjunction with the sale of other goods), the sale of wines, spirits, or other alcoholic liquors, in bottles or cases only, may be granted a licence for such sale by the Governor General. The fee for such licence shall not be less than L.E. 50 a year. The holder of such licence may be subjected to special restrictions as to the manner of conducting his business, and may be prohibited from selling to any specified persons or classes of persons.

6. If any premises licensed under this Ordinance are transferred in the course of a year the licence may be transferred to the transferee without payment, by order of the Mudir, if he approve of the transferee. *Transfer of licence to new licensee.*

7. The licence may be transferred from the licensed premises to other premises by order to be obtained from the Mudir. *Transfer of licence to new premises.*

8. The holder of a licence under this Ordinance shall not be entitled to renewal of his licence if the licensing authority deem it in the interests of public order or convenience to refuse to renew the licence. *Renewal of licence.*

The licensing authority shall not be bound to state its reasons for refusing to renew a licence.

9. Penalties under this Ordinance may be recovered, summarily or otherwise, before a Magistrate of the first or second class. *How penalties recoverable.*

10. This Ordinance shall not apply to the sale of merissa or native palm wine. *Saving.*

11. This Ordinance shall come into force on the day of its publication : but every person or company at the time carrying on a business which, under this ordinance, requires a licence shall be allowed the period of 14 days within which to apply for a licence. *Commencement of Ordinance.*

The importation of alcoholic liquors by any person or body of persons for his or their personal consumption and not for sale in accordance with the terms of a permit granted by the Governor General shall not be deemed to be a contravention of this Ordinance.

12. This Ordinance may be cited as the Licence (Liquor) Ordinance, 1899. *Short title.*

In connection with this Ordinance the following regulations were published in Sudan Gazette No. 31 of 1 January 1902.

REGULATIONS AS TO LIQUOR LICENCES.

Licences for the sale of alcoholic liquors will only be granted under the conditions following :—

1. If the Mudir is satisfied that there is a need for the grant of a licence.

2. If the Mudir is satisfied of the good character of the applicant.

3. If the Mudir is satisfied that the premises on which the business is to be carried on are suitable for the purpose.

4. The number of Licences in any place may not be increased except with the previous sanction of the Governor General.

5. A licence holder must furnish to the administrator or Mudir of the District or Mudiria through which any consignment of liquor for him enters the Sudan a true statement of the contents of the consignment and must obtain a permit for the same from such Administrator or Mudir. No consignment of liquor will be delivered by the Government Railway or Water Transport Service except upon the production of the said permit.

6. A licence holder shall keep proper books which may be examined at any time by the Mudir or his agent authorised in writing showing for every day (a) the amount of liquor imported by the licence holder (b) the amount of liquor sold to be consumed off the premises and the persons by whom purchased (c) the amount of liquor consumed on the premises.

7. No liquors of deleterious quality may be imported or sold. Any deleterious liquors may by order of a magistrate of the first or second class be seized and destroyed. Upon the written order of a magistrate of the first or second class a licence holder must supply to the police samples of all or any liquors in his possession.

8. A licence holder shall bind himself not to sell any alcoholic liquors to any native of the Sudan, or any British Soldier of the Army of Occupation who is not an officer. This prohibition shall not be construed to extend to the sale of alcoholic liquors to Sudanese Commissioned Officers.

9. A licence holder will be held responsible for the good order and conduct of his business and in particular he will be required to see (a) that no drunkeness is permitted on licensed premises (b) that no person in a state of intoxication is served with alcoholic liquors or allowed to remain on the premises (c) that no immorality or solicitation to immorality is permitted on the

premises (*d*) that the premises shall not be used as a gaming house and (*e*) that hasheesh and opium smoking are not allowed.

10. The times during which licensed premises in any place may be kept open for the sale of liquor are in the discretion of the Mudir. In the absence of any order from the Mudir, a licence holder shall not open his premises for the sale of alcoholic liquors before the hour of sunrise and shall not keep them open for the same purpose after the hour of midnight.

11. It shall be lawful for the police at any time to enter and search licensed premises.

12. Contravention of these regulations may be punished with revocation of licence or with fine not exceeding £E. 100, or both, but no revocation of a licence shall be effective unless passed or confirmed by the Mudir.

13. Penalties may be inflicted summarily or otherwise by a magistrate of the first or second class.

14. The grant of a licence for a year shall in no way constitute any right or claim to its renewal which is in the absolute discretion of the Mudir.

15. These regulations are issued under the Licence (Liquor) Ordinance 1899, and are in addition to and not in substitution *1899 No. 6.* for those contained in that Ordinance.

They repeal all other regulations previously issued.

In connection with the above regulations the following notices were published.

A.

Published in Sudan Gazette No. 32 of February 1902.

NOTICE AS TO LIQUOR LICENCES.

With reference to Clause 5, Regulations as to Liquor Licences (published in *Sudan Gazette* No. 31) notice is hereby given that all merchants, etc., importing liquor, must present detailed (in duplicate) invoices, giving particulars of quantity and nature of liquor in any particular consignment, to the Administrator Halfa or Suakin, according as liquor is imported via Halfa or Suakin.

These invoices (in duplicate) will be inspected and, if necessary, any part or the whole of the liquors mentioned therein will be examined by the Administrator who, after he has satisfied himself that the liquor is not deleterious, will endorse the invoices. On the presentation of the invoices thus endorsed to the Director of Sudan Government Railways, or other Official nominated by him at Halfa, or the Customs House Officer at Suakin, the consignment of liquor will be released and its import permitted.

One copy of the endorsed invoice should be filed with the liquor stock-book merchants are required by the regulations (clause 6) to keep up; this being the authority for the amount of liquor borne on their books.

Merchants who break up consignments of liquors for distribution to their agents at other centres, must obtain a permit (in duplicate) from the Mudir for this further consignment. A copy of this permit should be filed with the stock-books kept at those places, the other copy being retained as authority for the consignment.

Merchants and others importing liquor are therefore requested to do so on separate invoices, *i.e.* liquor should not be consigned and packed with other stores.

For a private consignment of liquor a permit is to be obtained from the Mudir or Administrator of the Province in which the individual resides. This permit should be presented with the invoice at Halfa or Suakin as the case may be, in the above mentioned manner. The Administrators of Halfa and Suakin have been sent a complete list of persons or firms holding Liquor Licences.

B.

Published in Sudan Gazette No. 35 of May 1902.

LIQUOR LICENCES.

Notice is hereby given that on and after 1st day of July, 1902, the following additional regulation for the sale of alcoholic liquors will come into force :—

No licence holder shall sell any alcoholic liquor contained in a bottle or other sealed vessel which does not bear a label with the name of the licence holder thereon.

1899 No. 7.

THE TAXATION (HOUSE TAX) ORDINANCE 1899.

Promulgated in Sudan Gazette No. 3 of 31 July 1899.

Amended by the Taxation (House Tax) Ordinance 1904 (Sud. Gaz. No. 66 of 1 September 1904) 1904 No. 5, and the Taxation (House Tax) Ordinance 1905 (Sud. Gaz. No. 73 of 1 March 1905) 1905 No. 4.

An Ordinance for regulating the House-Tax.

IT IS HEREBY ENACTED as follows:—

1. A tax, to be called "the house tax," shall be levied in such towns as the Governor General shall, from time to time, order by notice published in the "Sudan Gazette." *House tax to be levied.*

2. House tax shall subject to the exceptions hereinafter specified be paid in respect of all dwelling houses, hotels, stores, factories and other buildings, and shall be at the rate per annum of one twelfth of the annual rental value. *Tax to be levied on what property.*

The annual rental value of any premises is the annual sum which an ordinary tenant would pay for the premises, with their appurtenances, free from any restrictions as to user; but, in assessing the tax, no account shall be taken of furniture, or of machinery other than fixed machinery.

3. *The tax shall be paid in advance, by the owner of the premises assessed, by four equal instalments on the 1st day of January, the 1st day of April, the 1st day of July, the 1st day of October in every year, the first payment to be made on the first of such days after the publication of the first assessment list hereinafter mentioned.* *Mode of paying tax.*

§ *3. Repealed by the Taxation (House Tax) Ordinance 1905 (Sud. Gaz. No. 73 of 1 March 1905) 1905 No. 4 and other words substituted.*

4. The following buildings shall be exempt from house tax:— *Buildings exempted from tax.*

   (*a*) buildings the property of the Government, or of any Government Department:

   (*b*) Mosques, Churches, and all other buildings unproductive of revenue and used exclusively for religious or charitable purposes:

   (*c*) *premises in the occupation of the owner, of which the annual rental value does not exceed P.T. 500.*

Provided that the residence of a person following a religious life shall not be deemed to be used exclusively for religious purposes.

§ 4. *Words in italics rep. by the Taxation (House Tax) Ordinance 1904. (Sudan Gazette No. 66.) 1904 No. 5, and other words substituted.*

Unoccupied houses.

5. *Premises which have been unoccupied during three consecutive calendar months shall not again be liable to the payment of house tax until they are again occupied.*

§ 5. *Repealed by the Taxation (House Tax) Ordinance 1905 (Sud. Gaz. No. 73 of 1 March 1905) 1905 No. 4 and other words substituted.*

Assessment Commission.

6. The assessment of premises in each town shall be made by an Assessment Commission consisting of six persons namely: three Government Officials to be nominated by the Mudir, and three members to be chosen by the Mudir from a list of 12 owners of assessable property within the town, to be elected by the owners of assessable property.

The property of a member of the Assessment Commission shall be assessed by the other members of the Commission.

Publication of Assessment list.

7. As soon as may be after the completion of the assessment, an assessment list shall be published in the town.

Appeal.

8. An appeal shall lie from any assessment, at any time within three calendar months of the publication of an assessment list, to a Commission composed of the Mudir, the Inspector within whose district the town is situate and two owners to be chosen by the Mudir from the list mentioned in section 6 other than members of the Assessment Commission.

Appeals on behalf of the Government shall be brought by the Mamur or other prescribed official.

Costs of Appeal.

9. The Appellate Commission shall have power to award reasonable costs to a successful or against an unsuccessful appellant.

Revised assessment list.

10. In the month of December in every year, the Assessment Commission shall prepare and publish a revised assessment list, and for this purpose the Commission shall give public notice of the times of its sitting.

In the preparation of the revised list new buildings shall, and buildings not already assessed may, be included; but the assessment on a building already assessed shall not be altered unless it appear to the Assessment Commission that, owing to alterations in, or additions to, the premises, or for other reason, the rental value has increased, or the owner proves to the satisfaction of the Commission that the rental value has, for any reason, diminished.

No existing assessment shall be appealed against unless it has been increased, or unless the owner has applied to the Commission for a reduction.

11. The owner of any premises in or to which any alteration or addition is made, shall give notice of such alteration or addition to the Mamur or other prescribed official, not later than the 30th day of November next ensuing, under penalty of a fine not exceeding one year's house-tax on the premises. *Alteration of premises.*

12. If any part of the tax remain unpaid for one calendar month after the date at which it became payable, it may be recovered before a Magistrate of the first or second class, from the owner, as money due on a judgment. *Recovery of tax.*

13. Where there are more than two owners of any premises, or the owner or any one of the owners is not resident in the town, or is unknown, or cannot be found, and in any of such cases any part of the tax is in arrear for more than one calendar month, the Mudir may give notice to the occupant of the premises to pay his rent to the Government until such time as no part of the tax is in arrear; and until the Mudir rescinds such notice, the occupant shall be bound so to pay his rent, and his doing so shall be an answer to any action by the owner or owners for, or in respect of the rent so paid. *In certain cases rent to be paid to Government.*

Any rent so ordered to be paid to the Government may be recovered as a debt due, whenever it is more than one calendar month in arrear.

14. The Mudir shall issue regulations for the election of representatives of owners, and for all other purposes necessary or proper for giving effect to this Ordinance. *Mudir to issue Regulations.*

15. This Ordinance may be cited as the Taxation (House Tax) Ordinance 1899. *Short title.*

Pursuant to this Ordinance the following notice was published in Sudan Gazette No. 86 of 1 January 1906.

HOUSE TAX ORDINANCE 1899.

1899 No. 7.

The Notice published in accordance with the House Tax Ordinance 1899 in the Sudan Gazette No. 4 of September 9th 1899 ordering that House Tax should be levied in the towns therein named is hereby cancelled and in lieu thereof the Governor General in exercise of the powers conferred on him by section 1 of the said Ordinance hereby orders that House Tax shall be levied in the following cities and towns, that is to say Khartoum, Omdurman, Khartoum North, Suakin, Halfa and El Obeid.

1899 No. 8.

THE PUBLIC FERRIES ORDINANCE 1899.

Promulgated in Sudan Gazette No. 3. of 31 July 1899.
Repealed by the Public Ferries Ordinance 1900 (Sud. Gaz. No. 15 of 1 September 1900)
1900 No. 8.

1899 No. 9.

THE TAXATION (BOATS) ORDINANCE 1899.

Promulgated in Sud. Gaz. No. 3 of 31 July 1899.

An Ordinance for regulating the Boat Tax.

IT IS HEREBY ENACTED as follows :

Tax, rate of and how payable.

1. There shall be payable in respect of every boat plying upon the Nile or any of its tributaries within the Sudan, a boat tax, at the rate per annum of 2 P.T. per ardeb of the boat's carrying capacity. The tax shall be payable in advance by two equal half-yearly instalments, on the first day of January, and the first day of July in every year.

2. There shall be exempted from the boat tax :—   Exemptions.

(i) boats belonging to the Government,

(ii) licensed ferry-boats, and

(iii) boats whose owners are resident in Egypt and which do not ply above the Wadi Halfa cataract.

3. The first instalment of tax in respect of boats plying before   Tax when
the first day of July next shall be paid on or before that day ; in   payable.
respect of boats commencing to ply after the first day of July next,
the first instalment shall be paid before commencing to ply, and
shall be a proportionate amount only of the annual tax, corresponding to the then unexpired period of the current half-year.

4. Instalments of tax may be paid at any Mudiria.   Tax where payable.

5. Upon the first payment of tax, a certificate shall be given in   Certificate of
respect of the boat, stating its carrying capacity and that the tax   carrying
has been paid. The certificate shall be produced upon payment   capacity and of
of all future instalments, and notice of payment shall be endorsed   payment of tax.
thereon.

6. If a certificate be lost, a new certificate shall be granted at   Loss of
the Mudiria at which the last instalment of tax was paid, upon   Certificate.
payment of P.T. 5.

7. The boat certificate shall be produced upon demand to every   Production of
Magistrate or Police-Officer. Non-production of the certificate   Certificate.
shall be presumptive evidence that the tax has not been paid, and
shall be reported forthwith to the Mudir.

8. Every Mudir shall have power to arrest a boat, the certificate   Penalties.
of which is not produced or shows that any instalment of tax is
more than a calendar month in arrear. The Mudir shall, unless
good reason for non-payment be shewn, inflict a penalty not
exceeding three times the tax appearing to be in arrear.

The Mudir shall detain the boat in custody until the penalty be
paid.

9. If it subsequently appear that all instalments of tax have   Case in which
been paid, but that the certificate has been lost, the penalty shall   penalty
be repaid, less the price of a new certificate.   refunded.

10. If the penalty be not paid within three calendar months   Compulsory
of the date of arrest, the Mudir shall cause the boat to be sold by   sale of boat.

public auction, and, after deducting the costs of custody and of
the sale and the amount of the penalty, shall pay the balance of
the proceeds to the persons appearing to be entitled thereto.

For the purpose of ascertaining the persons entitled, the Mudir
shall retain the balance of the proceeds for 30 days, within which
time all claims thereon shall be made to him.

Short title.   **11.** This Ordinance may be cited as the Taxation (Boats)
Ordinance 1899.

1899 No. 10.

THE LICENCE (AUCTIONEERS AND PEDLARS) ORDINANCE 1899.

Promulgated in Sudan Gazette No. 3 of 31 July 1899.
*Repealed by the Auctioneer's, Broker's and Pedlar's Ordinance, 1905, (Sudan
Gazette No. 73 of 1 March 1905) 1905 No. 3.*

1899 No. 11.

THE SUDAN PENAL CODE.

*Printed separately and put in force in various Provinces and Districts of the
Sudan by Orders published from time to time in the " Sudan Gazette."*

In connection with this Ordinance the following Orders
have been issued :—

A.

*A Series of orders published in Sudan Gazette No. 5 of 2 October
1899, No. 21 of 1 March 1901 and No. 41 of November 1902 whereby
the Sudan Penal Code was put in force in the Provinces and Districts
therein respectively mentioned.*

B.

Published in Sudan Gazette No. 86 of January 1906.

SUDAN PENAL CODE, CODE OF CRIMINAL PROCEDURE, AND SUDAN CIVIL JUSTICE ORDINANCE 1900.

Whereas the Sudan Penal Code, the Code of Criminal Procedure, and the Sudan Civil Justice Ordinance 1900 have been put in force in various parts of the Sudan by notices published at various times in the Sudan Gazette and whereas by reason of the alteration of the Boundaries and names of the Provinces some confusion has been caused which it is desired to remove.

It is hereby ordered that :—

1. The Sudan Penal Code, the Code of Criminal Procedure and the Sudan Civil Justice Ordinance 1900 shall henceforth be deemed to have been in force since the 1st day of November 1903 and shall henceforth be in force in all Provinces of the Sudan except the Bahr el Ghazal Province.

2. Until further order the following provisions shall take effect :

(*a*) The provisions of the Code of Criminal Procedure and of the Sudan Civil Justice Ordinance 1900 relating to any act or proceeding to be done or taken by or before any Magistrate or Court shall be applied with such modifications not affecting the substance as, in the opinion of the Magistrate or Court, the circumstances may render necessary.

(*b*) The duties under the Code of Criminal Procedure of Police Officers and of Mamurs acting as Magistrates of the third class *and the duties under the Civil Justice Ordinance 1900 of Mamurs acting as Magistrates of the third class* shall be performed according to instructions conformable to the spirit of the Code of Criminal Procedure and the Civil Justice Ordinance 1900 to be issued, with due regard to all the circumstances of the case, by the Mudir or Governor of each Province or District.

Para 2 (b) the words in italics are contained in the original notice signed by the Governor General but were omitted in the Gazette.

3. As regards the Upper Nile and Mongalla Provinces proceedings shall be taken under the Code of Criminal Procedure in such cases only as shall be ordered in any general or special instruc-

5

tions from time to time issued by the respective Governors of these Provinces.

Any such instructions may provide for the omission of all or any part of any procedure which under the provisions of the Code of Criminal Procedure ought to take place before the trial of any accused person.

The Governors of these Provinces shall have power by any general or special instructions from time to time issued by them to order that any particular case or cases or any classes of cases shall not be dealt with under the Civil Justice Ordinance 1900.

4. Copies of the Sudan Penal Code, the Code of Criminal Procedure and the Sudan Civil Justice Ordinance 1900 shall be open for inspection at the Headquarter Office of each of the Provinces in which they are in force.

1899 No. 12.

THE SUDAN CODE OF CRIMINAL PROCEDURE.

Printed separately and put in force in various Provinces and Districts of the Sudan by Orders published from time to time in the " Sudan Gazette."

In connection with this Ordinance the following Orders have been issued :—

A.

A series of Orders published in Sudan Gazette No. 5 of 2 October 1899, No. 21 of 1 March 1901 and No. 41 of November 1902 whereby the Sudan Code of Criminal Procedure was put in force in the Provinces and Districts therein respectively mentioned.

B.

The order printed under the Sudan Penal Code (1899 No. 11) as Order B. supra p. 33.

1899 No. 13

THE WADI HALFA AND SUAKIN GENERAL ORDINANCE 1899.

Promulgated in Sudan Gazette No. 6 of 2 November 1899.

An Ordinance for regulating the application of general laws and regulations to the districts of Wadi Halfa and Suakin.

IT IS HEREBY ENACTED as follows :—

1. In the application of any general law, order or regulation to the district of Wadi Halfa or to the district of Suakin, the word " Mudir " shall be deemed to include " Governor or Administrator "; the word " Mudiria " shall be deemed to include a " Governorate " and the word " Province " shall be deemed to include a " District." *Interpretation of "Mudir," "Mudiria" and "Province."*

2. This Ordinance may be cited as " The Wadi Halfa and Suakin General Ordinance, 1899." *Short title.*

The districts of Wadi Halfa and Suakin are now 2nd class Mudirias (see Sudan Gazette No. 50 of 1 Aug. 1903).

1899 No. 14.

THE TAXATION OF HERDS ORDINANCE 1899.

Promulgated in Sud. Gaz. No. 7 of 2 December 1899.
Repealed by the Taxation of Animals Ordinance 1901 (Sud. Gaz. No. 26 of 1 August 1901) 1901 No. 7.

1899 No. 15.

THE MINING (PROSPECTING LICENCE) ORDINANCE 1899.

Promulgated in Sudan Gazette No. 8 of 2 January 1900.
Amended by the Revision Ordinance 1906 (Sud. Gaz. No. 92 of 1 April 1906).
1906 No. 1. and printed as amended.

An Ordinance regulating prospecting for metals, minerals, and precious stones, and prohibiting the working of mines without the authority of the Governor General.

WHEREAS all metals, minerals, mineral substances and precious stones, as well lying in under or on lands in private tenure as in under or on untenanted lands, are the property of the Government;

And whereas it is expedient to authorize prospecting for metals, minerals, mineral substances and precious stones, and to make such other regulations as to prospecting and mining as are hereinafter contained.

IT IS HEREBY ENACTED as follows:—

Short title.

1. This Ordinance may be cited as the Mining (Prospecting Licence) Ordinance 1899.

Sections 2 to 9 inclusive were repealed by the Revision Ordinance 1906 (1906 No. 1).

Offences and Penalties.

10.—(1) Any person, whether holding or not holding a Prospecting Licence, who alienates or exports or attempts to alienate or export any find, which he may have made of gold, silver, or precious stones, without having previously given notice of such find to the Governor General, shall forfeit the same and any money or profit received for the same, to the Government, and in addition shall be liable to a fine which may amount to L.E. 100, and in default of payment of the fine to imprisonment which may extend to three months.

(2) Any person who, whether upon land in private tenure or untenanted land, shall prospect for metals, minerals, mineral substances or precious stones, without a Prospecting Licence, or shall commence or carry on any mining operations without a mining lease or other sufficient authority from the Governor General, shall be liable to a fine which may amount to L.E. 100, and, in default of payment of the fine, to imprisonment, which may extend to three months.

Provided, nevertheless, that any owner of land may, upon giving notice to the Governor General, prospect upon the land in his tenure without a Prospecting Licence.

1900 No. 1.

THE WILD ANIMALS' PRESERVATION ORDINANCE 1900.

Promulgated in Sud. Gaz. No. 9 of 2 Feb. 1900.

Amended by the Wild Animals' Preservation Ordinance 1901 (Sud. Gaz. No. 19 of 1 January 1901) 1901 No. 3.

Repealed by the Preservation of Wild Animals' Ordinance 1901 (Sud. Gaz. No. 29 of 1 November 1901) 1901 No. 11. which was repealed by the Preservation of Wild Animals Ordinance 1903 (Sud. Gaz. No. 55 (Special) of December 1903) 1903 No. 9.

1900 No. 2.

THE SUDAN CIVIL JUSTICE ORDINANCE 1900.

Printed separately and put in force in various Provinces and Districts of the Sudan by Orders published from time to time in the " Sudan Gazette."

In connection with this Ordinance the following Orders have been issued:—

A.

A Series of Orders published in Sudan Gazette No. 10 of 1 April 1900, No. 21 of 1 March 1901 and No. 41 of November 1902 whereby the Sudan Civil Justice Ordinance 1900 was put in force in the Provinces and Districts therein respectively mentioned.

B.

The Order printed under the Sudan Penal Code (1899 No. 11) as Order B. supra p. 33.

Under the above Ordinance the following rules have been issued.

Published in Sud. Gaz. No. 11 of 1 May 1900.
Amended by Rule published in Sud. Gaz. No· 65 of 1 August 1905
and printed as amended.

1900 No. 2.

The following rules are hereby issued with the consent of the Governor General by the Judicial Commissioner, in exercise of the power vested in him under Section 135 of the Sudan Civil Justice Ordinance 1900 and every other power enabling him.

1. These rules may be cited as The Court Fees and Valuation of Suits Rules 1900.

PART I.

Court Fees.

1900 No. 2.

2. The fees prescribed by these rules shall be collected in the Courts established under the Sudan Civil Justice Ordinance 1900.

3. Fees proportionate to the value of the subject matter of the suit shall be collected upon the proceedings mentioned in clause 4 and shall be based upon the following scale :—

10 °/₀ upon the first fifty pounds :
8 °/₀ upon the second fifty pounds :
4 °/₀ upon the second and third hundred pounds :
2 °/₀ upon the other £E. 100 up to £E. 1000 :
1 °/₀ upon the surplus.

All fractions of a £E. for the purpose of calculating the value of a suit, shall be treated as an entire pound. The total percentage shall in no case exceed £E. 200.

ILLUSTRATIONS.

Value of Suit.	Scale Percentage.	£E.	M.
£E. 1 or any sum below	10 % of £E. 1	—	100
£E. 46.500	10 % of ,, 47	4	700
£E. 83.640	10 % of ,, 50	5	—
	8 % of ,, 34	2	720
		7	720
£E. 163	10 % of ,, 50	5	—
	8 % of ,, 50	4	—
	4 % of ,, 63	2	520
		11	520
£E. 429.250	10 % of ,, 50	5	—
	8 % of ,, 50	4	—
	4 % of ,, 200	..	—
	2 % of ,, 130	2	600
		19	600
£E. 1356	10 % of ,, 50	5	—
	8 % of ,, 50		—
	4 % of ,, 200	8	—
	2 % of ,, 700	14	—
	1 % of ,, 356	3	560
		34	560

4. Such fees shall be collected upon the proceedings and at the rates hereinafter mentioned, that is to say :

(1) For every plaint one quarter of the percentage according to the scale (hereinafter called the scale percentage).

(2) Upon passing judgment against a defendant in default of appearance, or upon passing judgment by consent of the parties before the Court has begun to hear the issues, one quarter of the scale percentage.

These fees will not be charged if a hearing fee has been paid.

(3) For every hearing, three quarters of the scale percentage. This fee will not be charged more than once in an action.

Hearing means the hearing of the suit, not the preliminary examination for settling the issues.

Where the fee mentioned in sub-section (4) has been paid the hearing fee will be reduced to one half the scale percentage.

(4) Upon every application by a defendant to set aside a judgment obtained against him in default of his appearance one quarter of the scale percentage.

(5) Upon the issue of every warrant of execution one half of the scale percentage. Provided that such fee shall not be less than P.T. 25 and shall be charged once only in every action in respect of the same decree.

(6) Upon every application for leave to appeal or notice of appeal to the Mudir one half of the scale percentage. Provided that such fee shall not be less than P.T. 25.

(7) Upon every application for leave to appeal or notice of appeal to the Judical Commissioner, three quarters of the scale percentage. Provided that such fee shall not be less than P.T. 50.

In fees below £E. 1 fractions of P.T. 1 shall count as P.T. 1, and in fees above £E. 1 fractions of P.T. 5 shall count as P.T. 5.

5. The following fees shall also be payable :—

	Where the subject matter of the suit	
	Does not exceed £E. 50.	Exceeds £E. 50.
	P.T.	P.T.
For every summons to a witness served by an Officer of the Court, if served within two kilometres of the Court house ...	5	15
For every kilometre beyond	1	1
But the total fee is not to exceed	15	25
In any proceedings where the number of defendants exceeds three, for every summons to a defendant beyond the number of three served by an Officer of the Court, if served within 2 kilometres of the Court house...	10	30
For every kilometre beyond	1	1
But the total fee is not to exceed	20	40

For every translation of a document other than a judgment made by an Officer of the Court at the request of any of the parties, for every 100 words P.T. 4.

For every plain copy of a document made by an Officer of the Court at the request of any of the parties, for every 100 words P.T. 2.

For certifying any copy of a document to be a correct copy, for every 100 words 1 P.T.

Any number of words less than 100 will be charged for in translation and copies as 100.

6. Upon the execution of decrees there shall also be payable such sums for the matters hereinafter mentioned as in the opinion of the Court have been actually and properly incurred, that is to say for the travelling expenses of the Officer executing the decree, for the wages of the man in possession, for the removal of the property to a place of safekeeping and for warehousing and taking charge of the same, for the advertisement of the auction and for the commission of an auctioneer.

7. The fees payable on any proceeding, shall, unless the Court otherwise orders, be paid in the first instance by the party on whose behalf the proceeding is taken, and the payment of any fee may be enforced in like manner as payment of a debt adjudged by the Court to be paid.

8. A receipt shall be given for all fees paid, and a statement of the fees paid in respect of any document shall be written on the document by the Officer by whom the fees are received, and shall be signed by him. A statement of the fee paid for the hearing shall be written at the beginning of the record of the hearing.

9. The Court may in its discretion remit the fees payable by any person whether a plaintiff or defendant upon proof of indigence, provided that it is satisfied that the applicant has a reasonable prospect of obtaining a decision in his favour.

10. The Court hearing an appeal, if it considers that the appeal was occasioned by the mistake of the Court from which the appeal was brought, may in its discretion order a return of the fee paid upon the notice of appeal or application for leave to appeal.

PART II.
Valuation of Suits.

11. The value of a suit shall be computed as follows:—

(1) In suits for money according to the amount claimed.

(2) In suits to establish a right to the payment of a periodical sum ten times the value of the amount claimed in one year.

(3) In suits for property having a market value, the value of such property at the date of presenting the claim.

Note. — *In a suit relating to land assessed for land tax, ten times the value of the land tax shall ordinarily be accepted as the value of the suit. In case however the magistrate has reason to believe that ten times the value of the land tax is materially above or below the true value he shall refer the question of value to one or more experts appointed by him whose decision shall be final.*

(4) In all suits other than for money or land assessed for land tax the plaintiff shall state the amount at which he values the relief sought and shall pay the fee according to such value, provided that if in the opinion of the Court the relief sought is undervalued and the plaintiff on being required by the Court to correct the valuation within a time to be fixed by the Court, fails to do so, the Court shall reject the plaint.

§ 11. *The words in italics were substituted for the rest of subsection (3) by the Rule of August 1904.*

12. If in any suit the value of the decree is in excess of the amount claimed or the amount at which the plaintiff valued the relief sought, the decree shall not be executed until the difference between the fees actually paid and the fees which would have been payable, had the claim or valuation of the relief sought comprised the whole of the value of the decree, shall have been paid to the proper officer.

For regulations concerning

(a) The Execution of Judgments of the Sudan Civil Courts in Egypt.

(b) The Execution of Judgments from another Province and Foreign Judgments.

(c) The method of serving Summonses of Sudan Courts in Egypt and Summonses of Egyptian Courts in the Sudan

see *Sudan Government Orders of 4th November 1904, Nos. 215, 216 and 222.*

1900 No. 3.

THE PUBLIC FERRIES ORDINANCE 1900.

Promulgated in the Sudan Gazette No. 15 of 1 September 1900.

An Ordinance for regulating Public Ferries.

IT IS HEREBY ENACTED as follows :—

1. This Ordinance may be cited as the Public Ferries Ordinance 1900.   Short title.

2. The Public Ferries Ordinance 1899 is hereby repealed, but such repeal shall not affect any right acquired or obligation undertaken by reason of any licence granted, or contract made by the Government under that Ordinance, nor the liability to prosecution for any offence against the Ordinance committed prior to its repeal.   Repeal. *1899 No. 8.*

3. No boat shall ply for hire upon any ferry declared by Government or by the Mudir to be a Public Ferry, otherwise than under a licence from the Mudir or other authority prescribed by the Governor General.   Ferry Boats to be licensed.

Subject to any regulations which may be issued by the Governor General, the Mudir or other prescribed authority shall issue regulations in respect of each ferry, prescribing the manner in which licences in respect thereof shall be granted and the conditions upon and subject to which licences shall be held.

4. The owner and every person in charge of a boat plying for hire upon a public ferry, otherwise than in virtue of a licence issued under the provisions of this Ordinance or of the Ordinance hereby repealed, may be fined a sum not exceeding P.T. 50 for each journey.   Penalty.

5. A special flag may be prescribed in any Mudiria which shall be carried by licensed ferry boats. Upon such flag being prescribed, the owner and every person in charge of a boat other than a licensed ferry boat flying this flag, may be fined a sum not exceeding P.T. 50 for each day upon which such flag is flown.   Flag.

6. Offences under this Ordinance may be tried summarily by any magistrate.

Trial of offences.   The Courts by which offences against the regulations relating to ferry boats may be tried, shall be prescribed by the regulations, but no sentence or forfeiture of a licence passed in virtue of such regulations shall be effective unless passed or confirmed by the Mudir, or other licensing authority.

1901 No. 1.

THE KHARTOUM, BERBER AND DONGOLA TOWN LANDS ORDINANCE 1901.

Promulgated in Sudan Gazette No. 19 of 1 January 1901.

An Ordinance for extending the time within which allottees of land at Khartoum and Berber are required to erect buildings.

IT IS HEREBY ENACTED as follows:—

Short title.   1. This Ordinance may be cited as the Khartoum, Berber, and Dongola Town Lands Ordinance 1901.

Khartoum, Berber & Dongola Town Lands Ordinance 1899. § 10 amended.

1899 No. 1.

2. The time within which under Section 10 of the Khartoum, Berber, and Dongola Town Lands Ordinance 1899, an allottee of land within the towns of Khartoum or Berber is under an obligation to erect a building on the land allotted to him is extended as follows:— If the allotment was made, or notice that the Commission was ready to fix the allotment was given on or before the 31st December, 1900, the time is extended to the 31st December, 1902: if notice that the Commission is ready to fix the allotment is given for the first time after the 31st December, 1900, the time is extended to two years from the date of such notice.

Notices to allottees.   3. Notices issued by any of the Commissions constituted under the Khartoum, Berber, and Dongola Town Lands Ordinance 1899 to allottees shall be sufficiently given by posting the same upon the official notice board of the town mamuria, and every such notice shall be deemed to have been communicated to the allottees or allottee concerned upon the day that it is so posted.

NOTE. — *See the notes and Proclamations printed with the Khartoum, Berber, and Dongola Town Lands Ordinance 1899. (1899 No. 1) supra p. 1.*

1901 No. 2.

THE ROYALTY ON GUM ETC. ORDINANCE 1901.

(Sudan Gazette No. 19).
Repealed by The Royalties on Gum etc. Ordinance 1904. (Sudan Gazette No. 66 of 1 September 1904). 1904 No. 7.

1901 No. 3.

THE WILD ANIMALS PRESERVATION ORDINANCE 1901.

(Sudan Gazette No. 19).
Repealed by The Preservation of Wild Animals Ordinance 1901. (Sudan Gazette No. 29 of 1 November 1901). 1901 No. 11.

1901 No. 4.

THE EGYPTIAN JUDGMENTS ORDINANCE 1901.

Promulgated in Sudan Gazette No. 23 of 1 May 1901.
Amended by the Egyptian Judgments Ordinance 1904. (Sudan Gazette No. 62 of 1 May 1904). 1904 No. 3. which extended the provisions of this ordinance to Judgments of the Egyptian Mixed Tribunals.

The Egyptian Judgments Ordinance 1901.

WHEREAS cases have arisen in which judgments have been obtained before *the* Egyptian *Native* Tribunals against persons residing in the Sudan or holding property therein and it is expedient that such recognition should be given to such judgments in the Sudan as shall prevent needless multiplicity of suits:

Words in italics repealed by Egyptian Judgments Ordinance 1904 (Sudan Gazette No. 62). 1904 No. 3.

NOW IT IS HEREBY ENACTED as follows :—

Short title.
1. This Ordinance may be cited as the Egyptian Judgments Ordinance 1901.

In what districts applicable.
2. This Ordinance shall apply to those parts of the Sudan only in which the Sudan Civil Justice Ordinance 1900, shall for the time being be in force.

To what judgments not applicable.
3. (1) Nothing in this Ordinance shall apply to any judgment of an Egyptian Court being

(*a*) a judgment purporting to adjudicate upon the title to, or the right to the possession of immovable property elsewhere than in Egypt, or to adjudicate as to any mortgage or charge thereon or to give redress for any injury in respect of such immovable property ; or

(*b*) a judgment against the Sudan Government or against any officer of that Government in respect of any official act as such officer; or

(*c*) a judgment passed in exercise of bankruptcy jurisdiction.

Meaning of a " final judgment."
(2) For the purpose of this Ordinance "a final judgment" means a judgment which is final and unalterable in the Court by which it was pronounced, whether an appeal against it lies to another Court or not.

Effect of final judgment pronounced by Egyptian Court.
4. Every final judgment pronounced by an *Egyptian Native Court* in any civil or commercial proceedings shall, subject to the provisions and exceptions hereinafter contained, have the effects following, so long as it remains in force :—

(*a*) It shall be conclusive evidence, in every proceeding before a Civil Court in the Sudan between the same parties in the same right or between parties claiming under them, of every matter decided by it:

(*b*) Save so far as it appears that the judgment proceeded upon a rule of law or of procedure which prevented the proceeding from being brought in the Court by which such judgment was given, but which did not at the same time extinguish the claim in respect of which the proceeding was sought to be brought, it shall be a complete bar, as between the same parties in the same right or between parties claiming under them, to any proceeding before any Civil Court in the Sudan in respect of the same claim.

§ 4. *Words in italics rep. by Egyptian Judgments Ordinance 1904 (Sudan Gazette No. 62). 1904 No. 3. and other words substituted.*

5. Every person entitled to the benefit, as against any other person who is resident in the Sudan or has property therein, of a final judgment pronounced by an *Egyptian Native Court* in any civil or commercial proceeding may, if such judgment is executory in Egypt, bring an action on the judgment against such other person before the Court of the Mudir of the Province in which such other person is resident or in which any property of his is situate.

Action on a judgment pronounced by Egyptian Court.

Such action shall, subject to the provisions of this Ordinance, be in the same form as in an ordinary case within the jurisdiction of the Court, and the judgment of the Court, if it be in favour of the plaintiff, shall be framed to give him, as nearly as the differences between the law and procedure in Egypt and Sudan will admit, the relief to which he would be entitled in Egypt.

§ 5. *Words in italics rep. by Egyptian Judgments Ordinance 1904 (Sudan Gazette No. 62). 1904 No. 3 and other words substituted.*

6. (1) If the executory judgment of an Egyptian Court mentioned in the last preceding section be for a debt or other definite sum of money, the judgment-holder shall, subject to the provisions hereinafter contained, be entitled to execution of the judgment in the Sudan in the same manner as if the judgment were a judgment of the Court of the Mudir of the Province in which the person bound by the judgment is resident or in which any property of his is situate, without it being necessary to bring a new action on the judgment.

Executory judgment of Egyptian Court for a debt.

Nevertheless, before causing execution to issue, the Mudir shall issue a summons in the manner prescribed for the issue of summonses to defendants by the Civil Justice Ordinance 1900, directing the person against whom execution is sought to show cause why execution should not issue.

(2) This section shall apply equally to a judgment pronounced by an Egyptian Court in a criminal proceeding and executory in Egypt, in so far as the judgment orders the payment of a definite sum of money.

When judgment part satisfied.

7. Where it appears that a judgment sought to be enforced under section 5 or section 6 of this Ordinance has been in part satisfied in Egypt, these sections shall apply as if the judgment were for such part of the judgment only as has not been satisfied.

Requisites in judgment.

8. In order that the judgment of an Egyptian *Native* Tribunal may have in the Sudan the effect mentioned in sections 4, 5 and 6 of this Ordinance it must appear from the judgment or be otherwise shewn either that,

(1) the party against whom or against whose representatives it is sought to use or enforce the judgment was plaintiff in the proceeding before the Egyptian Tribunal or being a defendant appeared therein : or that.

(2) the citation was served on him personally in Egypt : or that,

(3) he was *an Egyptian local subject* domiciled or ordinarily resident in Egypt : or that.

(4) the action related to property, whether movable or immovable, situate in Egypt; or that.

(5) the cause of action arose from a contract entered into in Egypt or intended to be there executed wholly or in part, or from acts which wholly or in part, were done in Egypt.

In the cases 3, 4 and 5 it must also appear or be shewn that citation was regularly served according to the rules laid down by the Egyptian *Native* Codes.

§ 8. *Words in italics rep. by Egyptian Judgments Ordinance 1904 (Sudan Gazette No. 62). 1904 No. 3.*

Judgment shall be verified.

9. Every judgment sought to be used or enforced in virtue of this Ordinance shall, unless it be admitted by the party against whom it is sought to be used or enforced, be verified by a true copy of the judgment certified under the seal of the Egyptian Ministry of Justice.

Where it is sought to enforce the judgment under section 5 or section 6 of this Ordinance, it shall further require to be certified under the seal of the said Ministry of Justice that the judgment is executory in Egypt.

Judgment when defendant not cited.

10. Every judgment of an Egyptian Court which it is sought to use or enforce in accordance with the provisions of this Ordinance, may, if it appear that the judgment was pronounced against a defendant who did not appear before the Egyptian Court and on whom citation in the proceeding before the Egyptian Court was not personally served in Egypt, be attacked by the party against whom it is sought to use or enforce the judgment, on the ground that it was obtained by fraud.

11. Notwithstanding that the judgment states that the defendant appeared before the Egyptian Court or the citation was served upon him personally in Egypt it shall be open to the person against whom it is sought to use or enforce the judgment, to show, for the purpose of the last preceding section, that the defendant did not in fact appear or that citation was not in fact so served.

To what extent the judgment is evidence.

In all other respects the judgment shall be conclusive evidence of everything stated therein which shows that it falls within the provisions of section 8 of this Ordinance or within any of them.

12. Any Civil Court in the Sudan may, upon such terms as it may think fit as to costs or otherwise, stay the progress of any proceedings before it, in which an Egyptian judgment is pleaded in virtue of the provisions of section 4 of this Ordinance or of any proceeding for enforcing an Egyptian judgment under section 5 or section 6 if it appears that the judgment is open to appeal or other recourse in Egypt.

Stay of proceedings when Egyptian Judgment open to appeal.

13. Where in the course of any proceeding before a Civil Court in the Sudan it appears that proceedings are pending before an Egyptian *Native* Court the judgment in which, if already delivered would or might be binding on the Court under the provisions of section 4 of this Ordinance, the Court may stay the progress of the proceeding before it, pending the decision of the Egyptian Court, upon such terms as it may think fit as to costs or otherwise.

Stay of proceedings when case pending in Egypt.

§ 3. *Word in italics rep. by Egyptian Judgments Ordinance 1904 (Sudan Gazette No. 62.) 1904 No. 3.*

Judgments of the Religious Courts.

14. The judgments of the Egyptian religious Courts shall be recognized and enforced in the Sudan in like manner and subject to the like conditions, so far as the differences in law and procedure between the Civil and Religious Courts in the Sudan and Egypt

Judgments of Egyptian religious courts.

respectively permit as is hereinbefore provided with reference to the judgments of the *Egyptian Native Tribunals.*

§ 14. *Words in italics rep. by Egyptian Judgments Ordinance 1904 (Sudan Gazette No. 62). 1904 No. 3. and other words substituted.*

Rules.

15. The Judicial Commissioner and Grand Kadi each as regards the Courts subordinate to him may from time to time with the consent of the Governor General make rules and prescribe forms consistent with this Ordinance for purpose of carrying into effect the provisions of this Ordinance.

1901 No. 5.

THE TRIBUTE ORDINANCE 1901.
Promulgated in Sudan Gazette No. 26 of 1 August 1901.

An Ordinance for regulating the levying of tribute.

Short title.

1. This Ordinance may be cited as the Tribute Ordinance 1901.

By whom tribute payable.

2. Tribute shall be payable annually by all nomad tribes within the limits of the Sudan.

Assessment of tribute.

3. The amount of tribute shall be assessed annually by each Mudir for every nomad tribe within his Mudiria and such tribute shall be payable upon the day or days which shall be fixed by the Mudir for each tribe.

In the event of a nomad tribe being within the limits of two or more Mudirias the assessment shall be made by such Mudir as the Governor General directs.

Collection of tribute.

4. Subject to the approval of the Governor General, Mudirs may make and publish regulations as to the collection, apportionment and payment of the tribute for the tribes within their respective Mudirias or any of them.

Duty of Sheikhs.

5. Subject to such regulations, if any, the Sheikh of each tribe shall be responsible for the collection of the tribute and that the

same is apportioned fairly amongst the members of the tribe having regard to their means.

6. Payment of tribute shall be enforced against the members of a defaulting tribe individually, or the tribe as a whole, in such manner, and by such means as the Governor General may think fit.

Enforcement of payment.

1901 No. 6.

THE LAND TAX ORDINANCE 1901.

Promulgated in Sudan Gazette No. 26 of 1 August 1901.
Repealed by the Land Tax Ordinance 1905 (Sud. Gaz. No. 82 of 1 October 1905)
1905 No. 11.

1901 No. 7.

THE TAXATION OF ANIMALS ORDINANCE 1901.

Promulgated in Sudan Gazette No. 26 of 1 August 1901.
Amended by the Taxation of Animals Ordinance 1903 (Sud. Gaz. No. 45 of March 1903.) 1903 No. 2.

An Ordinance for imposing and regulating a tax upon animals.

1. This Ordinance may be cited as the Taxation of Animals Ordinance 1901.

Short title.

2. A tax shall be payable in respect of horses, camels, donkeys, cattle, sheep and goats in such parts of the Sudan as shall from time to time be notified by the Governor General in the Sudan Gazette.

Animals in respect of which tax payable.

3. The tax shall be payable annually on such day or days as shall be fixed by each Mudir for his Mudiria at the following rates, that is to say:—

Rates of tax.

For each horse ...   .   P.T.   30.
For each camel ...   .   P.T.   20.
For each donkey or mule   ...   P.T.   3.
For each head of cattle   ...   P.T.   5.
For each sheep ...   .   P.T.   1.
For each goat ...   .   Mill.   5.

or at such other rates as shall from time to time be notified by the Governor General in the Sudan Gazette.

In Sud. Gaz. No. 43 of January 1903 it was notified that the tax upon horses was altered from P.T. 30 to P. T. 3.

Exemptions.   4. There shall be exempted from the tax—

(1) All animals belonging to a tribe which pays tribute or to a member of such tribe who is liable to contribute to such tribute.

(2) Young immature animals.

(3) All oxen ordinarily used for irrigation by Sakias.

§ 4 extended by taxation of Animals Ordinance 1903 (Sudan Gazette No. 45). 1903 No. 2. by the addition of the following clauses.

(4) All animals belonging to the Government or to any local public authority.

(5) Any animals belonging to officers or officials of the Egyptian or Sudan Governments or public servants as defined by the Sudan Penal Code for which forage or forage allowance is drawn from either Government or which in the opinion of the Governor General are reasonably necessary for the performance of their duties as public servants by such persons and shall by notice issued in the Sudan Gazette be declared by the Governor General to be exempt.

Assessments to be annual.   5. Assessments shall be made annually under the authority of each Mudir of the amount of tax payable by every owner of the animals hereby taxed in his Mudiria.

Appeal.   6. An appeal against every assessment under section 5 shall lie to the Mudir or other Magistrate appointed by him to try appeals at any time within 14 days of the notification of publication of the assessment. Subject to any alterations made upon appeal, the assessment shall be conclusive as to the amount of the tax payable by each owner.

Penalty.   7. If the tax is not paid in any year within 15 days after the date or dates fixed by the Mudir, the Mudir shall have power to charge the defaulting owner or owners, in lieu of the original tax, with a penalty of three times the amount thereof. Such penalty shall be recoverable by seizure and sale of a sufficient number of the animals under a warrant which may be issued without trial by the Mudir or any magistrates authorised by him in this behalf subject to a right of appeal to the Mudir or magistrate within seven days after the seizure or as a fine imposed under the Sudan Penal Code.

Repeal.
8. The "Taxation of Herds Ordinance 1899" is hereby cancelled. *1899 No. 14.*

1901 No. 8.

THE WOODS AND FORESTS ORDINANCE 1901.
Promulgated in Sud. Gaz. No. 26 of 1 August 1901.

An Ordinance for regulating Woods and Forests.

IT IS HEREBY ENACTED as follows :—

1. This Ordinance may be cited as the Woods and Forests Ordinance 1901. Short title.

2. No wood or forest in Sudan territory on the banks of any navigable river or stream, or within five miles of any such river or stream, may be cut, nor may wood or timber from the same be sold without a licence from the Mudir or other public officer authorized by the Governor General. Licence necessary for cutting wood.

3. Provided nevertheless that there is excepted from the provision contained in the last clause :— Exception.

(a) The cutting and sale of wood for domestic purposes.

(b) The cutting of wood and timber by natives for their own use in any way in which they have hitherto been accustomed to use it.

(c) The cutting of wood and timber for the Government and the sale thereof to the same.

4. Subject to any regulations which may be issued by the Governor General, licences under this Ordinance shall be issued by Mudirs upon payment of such fees, if any, and subject to such conditions as they may decide. Licence to be issued by Mudirs.

Penalties.

5. Any person who contravenes this Ordinance or any regulations which may be issued under this Ordinance shall be liable to a fine not exceeding £E. 25 for each day on which the offence is committed and to imprisonment which may extend to three months.

All timber and wood in respect of which the provisions of this Ordinance or of any regulations issued thereunder are contravened shall be liable to be confiscated and may be seized without any adjudication subject to right of appeal to a magistrate of the first or second class.

If the person convicted is the holder of a licence, his licence may be forfeited by the Licencing Authority.

In connection with this Ordinance the following Rules were published in Sudan Gazette No. 46 of April 1903.

Forest Administration Rules.

The following rules regarding Forest Administration are published for general information.

Felling trees for timber or firewood.

1. All persons desiring to fell trees for timber or firewood within any Government Forest shall apply for permit to the Mudir or Administrator (as the case may be) of the Province within which they intend to fell or to any Inspector or other person empowered in that behalf by such Mudir or Administrator. It shall not be necessary to make any such application on stamped paper.

Contents of application.

2. Every such application shall state :—

(a) The name and residence of the applicant.

(b) The place or places at which he desires to fell.

(c) What kind or kinds of trees he desires to fell.

(d) The purpose for which the trees are to be felled *i.e.* whether for timber or firewood and if for timber whether for boat building or for household or agricultural requirements or for sale and if for firewood whether for use or for sale.

(e) The quantity to be felled to be shown as follows :—

(i) If timber is required for boat building by reference to the ardebage of the boat or boats proposed to be built.

(ii) If timber is required for any other purpose by reference to the number of trees to be felled.

(iii) If trees are to be felled for firewood by reference to the number of kantars of firewood required.

(*f*) The time for which a permit is required with dates of commencement and expiration.

3. No permit will be granted for a period longer than one year in the case of firewood for domestic consumption or for a period longer than three months in any other case, provided that the Mudir or Administrator of the province in which the trees are to be felled or any Inspector or other person authorized by such Mudir or Administrator in this behalf may on sufficient cause being shown grant an extension of the period during which any such permit shall be valid. *Length of permit.*

4. The felling or destruction of trees by means of fire is absolutely prohibited. *Felling trees by fire prohibited.*

5. It shall not be lawful to fell trees or lop branches in Government Forests for use as fodder, except in areas selected and proclaimed for that purpose by the Mudir or Administrator of each province. *Felling or lopping trees for fodder prohibited.*

1901 No. 9.

THE CIVIL JUDGES ORDINANCE 1901.

Promulgated in Sudan Gazette No. 26 of 1 August 1901.

An Ordinance for regulating the position of Civil Judges.

WHEREAS a Civil Judge has been appointed, and it is desired to regulate his position, and that of other Civil Judges who may hereafter be appointed.

IT IS HEREBY ENACTED as follows:—

1. This Ordinance may be cited as the Civil Judges Ordinance 1901. *Short title.*

2. A Civil Judge shall be a magistrate of the first class both under the Code of Criminal Procedure and the Sudan Civil *Position and powers of Civil Judges.*

Justice Ordinance, and shall have all the Judicial powers of a Mudir in all civil and criminal matters which may be referred to him, whether by a special or general order, by the Mudir having jurisdiction in respect of the said matters.

1901 No. 10.

THE CATTLE PLAGUE ORDINANCE 1901.

Promulgated in Sudan Gazette No. 28 of 1 October 1901.

An Ordinance for dealing with the Cattle Plague.

Duty of possessor of affected cattle.

1. Every person having in his possession or under his charge any cattle affected or suspected to be affected with cattle plague or any other contagious disease shall (*a*) immediately give notice thereof to the nearest Government Official (*b*) as far as possible keep any affected animal separate from any other animal not so affected.

Duty of Sheikhs and Omdas.

2. All Sheikhs and Omdas shall be responsible for giving notice of the out-break of disease among the cattle of any of their people and will be held liable to the same extent as the persons mentioned in clause 1 hereof for giving such notice as therein mentioned.

Duty of Mudir.

3. The Mudir on receiving information of the out-break of disease shall thereupon take steps with the assistance of the Principal Veterinary Officer to ascertain whether the disease reported be cattle plague.

Mudir may declare a district an infected area.

4. On the existence of cattle plague being ascertained, the Mudir shall have power under the advice of the Principal Veterinary Officer (*a*) to declare any place or district within his jurisdiction an infected area (*b*) to extend contract or otherwise alter the limits of an infected area (*c*) to declare an infected area to be free from cattle plague which shall thereupon cease to be an infected area.

Regulations for infected areas.

5. When any place or district has been declared an infected area the following regulations shall be in force:—

(1) No cattle nor the bones, skins, horns, hoofs, or any other part of cattle shall be removed out of, into, or within an infected area without the leave in writing of the Mudir.

(2) Cattle owners shall use their utmost endeavours to keep their own herds from mixing with those of others and shall as far as possible water them elsewhere than at the Nile or other common watering place and all Sheikhs and Omdas shall use their utmost endeavours to see that these regulations are carried out.

(3) Owners of more than 10 head of cattle, when directed by the Mudir, shall immediately report to the Zaptia the arrangements made for feeding and watering their cattle.

6. The Government and its Officials shall have power to inspect, treat, and inoculate any cattle thought fit, and all Omdas, Sheikhs, and cattle owners shall give all possible assistance to the Government and its Officials in carrying out such work, whether within or without an infected area. **Power of Government to inspect.**

7. The Mudir, under the advice of the Principal Veterinary Officer, shall have power with a view to carrying out the objects and provisions of this Ordinance to do all or any of the following things:— **Power of Mudir.**

(1) To declare a place or district an infected area.

(2) To prohibit or regulate the movements of cattle and persons into, within, or out of an infected area.

(3) To prescribe and regulate the isolation or separation of cattle in an infected area and the inoculation or other treatment of cattle whether in or out of an infected area.

(4) To prohibit or regulate the removal of carcases, fodder, litter, dung, or other things into, within or out of an infected area.

(5) To prescribe and regulate the destruction by fire or otherwise, burial, disposal, or treatment of carcases, fodder, litter, dung, or other things being in an infected area or removed thereout.

(6) To prescribe and regulate the cleansing and disinfection of an infected area or any part thereof.

(7) To prescribe and regulate the disinfection of the clothes of persons coming in contact with or employed about diseased or

. 8

suspected animals, or being in an infected area and the use of precautions against the spreading of disease by such persons.

(8) To prohibit the digging up of carcases which have been buried.

(9) To prohibit or regulate the exposure of diseased or suspected cattle in markets or other places where they are commonly exposed for sale.

(10) To prohibit or regulate the sending, carrying, driving, or leading diseased or suspected cattle, or of dung, or other things likely to spread disease on railways, roads, or rivers.

(11) To prescribe and regulate the seizure, detention and disposal of any diseased or suspected cattle exposed, carried, kept or otherwise dealt with in contravention of this Ordinance, or of an order of the Mudir, and to prescribe and regulate the liability of the owner or consignor or consignee of such cattle to the expenses connected with the seizure, detention and disposal thereof.

(12) To prescribe and regulate the issue and production of licences respecting movement and removal of cattle and things.

(13) To prohibit or regulate the holding of markets and sales of cattle.

(14) To prescribe and regulate the cleansing and disinfection of places used for the holding of markets or sales of cattle or for lairage of cattle, and of yards, sheds, stables, vessels, vehicles, pens and other places used for cattle whether the same are in an infected area or not.

(15) To prescribe and regulate the marking of animals.

(16) To do or order such other things of the same nature as the Principal Veterinary Officer considers expedient.

Extension of Ordinance by proclamation.

8. The Governor General may at any time by proclamation extend the provisions of this Ordinance or any of them so as to include any other contagious disease of cattle and so as to be applicable to sheep, goats, swine or any other four-footed animals.

Penalties.

9. Persons failing or refusing to carry out any of the provisions of this Ordinance or any orders or regulations made hereunder shall be liable on conviction to a fine not exceeding £E. 200 or imprisonment not exceeding one year or both.

10. Offences under this Ordinance may be tried by a Magistrate Trial of offences. of the second class or any Court having higher powers.

11. This Ordinance may be cited as the Cattle Plague Ordin- Short title. ance 1901.

In virtue of § 8 of this Ordinance the following Proclamation was promulgated in Sudan Gazette No. 35 of May 1902 :—

Proclamation.

Whereas under the Cattle Plague Ordinance 1901, I have power 1901 No. 10. to extend the provisions of the said Ordinance to sheep, goats or other four-footed animals.

And whereas a contagious disease affecting goats has broken out in the Mudiria Sennar and contagious diseases may break out among sheep, camels, horses or asses which will cause great loss to the people if they are not stopped as soon as possible.

Now therefore I proclaim that henceforward all the provisions of the Cattle Plague Ordinance shall apply to goats, sheep, camels, horses and asses, and all persons must :

(1) Give notice immediately of the outbreak of any contagious disease among all such animals in their possession to the nearest Official of the Government, and—

(2) must keep the sick animals apart from the healthy ones, and obey all such orders as Mudirs shall give in this matter. And all Mashaikh and Omad are warned that they must see their people obey this proclamation in order that the Government may so far as possible prevent the spread of disease among animals and the people suffering loss thereby.

1901 No. 11.

THE PRESERVATION OF WILD ANIMALS ORDINANCE 1901.

(Sud. Gaz. No. 29).
Repealed by the Preservation of Wild Animals Ordinance 1903 (Sud. Gaz. No. 55. (Special) of December 1903) 1903 No. 9.

1901 No. 12.

THE MUNICIPAL COUNCILS ORDINANCE 1901.

Promulgated in Sud. Gaz. No. 29 of 1 November 1901.

An Ordinance empowering the establishment of Municipal Councils in the Sudan.

Power of Governor General to establish Municipal Council.

1. The Governor General shall have power to establish a Municipal Council in such towns of the Sudan as he shall think fit.

Constitution of Council.

2. A Council shall be a Corporation with power to hold land and shall consist of not less than five members to be appointed by the Governor General, but there shall always be included among such members the Mudir for the time being of the Province in which the town is situated or a representative nominated by him who shall be president, the Medical Officer for the time being of the town if one exists, one notable and one merchant of the town.

Vacation of Office.

3. A member of a Council shall ipso facto vacate his Office on the occurrence of any of the following events :—

(1) Death.

(2) Departure to reside out of the district.

(3) Notice, in writing to the President, of his resignation.

(4) The acceptance of any Office of profit under the Council.

(5) Notice by the Governor General to be published in the *Sudan Gazette* of the cancellation of his appointment.

4. A Council shall be charged with the following duties, subject in any particular case to such additions, modifications, and omissions, as the Governor General shall determine :—

(1) The lighting of the town.

(2) The enforcement of building and sanitary regulations for the time being in existence.

(3) The payment of policemen and ghaffirs.

(4) The cleansing, watering, making and maintenance of the public streets.

(5) The control of markets and slaughter-houses.

(6) The control or prevention of dangerous and noxious trades.

(7) The prevention of adulteration of articles of sale and of the sale of unsound, or unwholesome food or drink.

(8) The inspection of weights and measures.

(9) The authorization and regulation of cemeteries.

(10) The enforcement of vaccination.

(11) The granting of such licences for vehicles, drivers, shoe-blacks, porters, street-vendors, and others, as the Council may determine.

(12) Such other duties as the Governor General· shall from time to time prescribe.

5. A Council shall have all powers necessary for the carrying out of its duties, including a power to levy rates on occupiers of all houses, or lands within the municipality, a power, with the consent of the Governor General, to borrow money for municipal purposes, to be charged upon the municipal revenues or property, a power with the like consent to purchase and sell land, a power to charge fees for licences, and the inspection of weights and measures, and a power to make such by-laws to be approved before coming into force by the Governor General for the carrying out of their duties in their particular municipalities, and for levying and recovery of fines for breach of such by-laws, or of any ordinance with the enforcement of which the Council is charged. *Powers of Council.*

6. The revenue of the Council shall consist of — *Revenue of Council.*

(1) The rates levied by the Council under its powers.

(2) The fines inflicted for breach of any of the ordinances and regulations which the Council is charged with enforcing.

(3) Any fees charged by the Council in respect of any of the matters hereby entrusted to it.

7. This Ordinance may be cited as the Municipal Councils Ordinance 1901. *Short title.*

1901 No. 13.

THE CONTRABAND GOODS ORDINANCE 1901.

Promulgated in Sud. Gaz. No. 31 of 1 January 1901.

*Amended by the Revision Ordinance 1906 (Sudan Gazette No. 92 of 1 April 1906)
1906 No. 1. and printed as amended.*

An Ordinance for Preventing and Regulating the Introduction and Manufacture of Contraband Goods.

IT IS HEREBY ENACTED as follows:

Prohibition and restrictions on imports and manufactures.

1. The goods enumerated and described in the following table of prohibitions and restrictions are hereby prohibited to be imported or brought into the Sudan, or made or manufactured in the Sudan save as hereby excepted, and if any goods so enumerated and described shall be imported or brought into the Sudan *or made or manufactured in the Sudan* contrary to the prohibitions or restrictions contained therein, such goods shall be forfeited and may be destroyed or otherwise disposed of as the Governor General shall from time to time direct, and in addition, the means of transport of such goods may be confiscated and all persons, whether principals or not, concerned in importing *or making or manufacturing* such contraband goods may be punished by fine not exceeding £E. 500 or imprisonment for a term not exceeding seven years or both.

A Table of Prohibitions and Restrictions.

(1) False or counterfeit money, weights or measures, whether of Egypt or of any other country.

(2) Prints, paintings, photographs, books, cards, lithographic or other engravings or any other articles which are indecent, obscene, or calculated to throw contempt on the Moslem or Christian religions.

(3) Infected cattle or other animals or the carcases, hides, skins, horns, or hoofs, or any other animals or parts thereof which the Governor General may by order prohibit in order to prevent the dissemination of any contagious disease.

(4) Fire-arms, ammunition, gunpowder, explosives and materials for the manufacture of gunpowder and explosives except under a

Government permit or the provisions and regulations of any Ordinance for the time being in force relative to the importation or carrying of the same.

(5) Wines, spirits, or any alcoholic liquors, other than perfumed or methylated spirit, except under the provisions and regulations of any Ordinance for the time being in force for regulating and licensing the sale of the same, but this prohibition shall not extend to the making of fermented native liquors unless the same are produced by a process of distillation or are of a peculiarly injurious nature.

(6) Arsenic and its preparations, prussic acid, cyanides of potassium and all metallic cyanides, strychnine and all poisonous vegetable alkaloids and their salts, emetic tartar, aconite and its preparations, corrosive sublimate, cantharides, savin and its oil, ergot of rye and its preparations, cannabis indica (Indian Hemp or Hasheesh), oxalic acid, chloroform, belladonna and its preparations, essential oil of almonds unless deprived of its prussic acid, opium and all preparations of opium or of poppies, unless the same or any of them are consigned to or made grown or manufactured by a duly qualified medical man, a person licenced to sell poisons or any other persons specially permitted by the Governor General.

(7) Such other articles as the Governor General may from time to time prohibit.

§ 1. *Words in italics inserted by the Revision Ordinance 1906. (Sudan Gazette No. 92 of 1 April 1906) 1906 No. 1.*

Subsection (5). See the Native Liquors Ordinance 1903 (Sudan Gazette No. 49 of 1 July 1903) 1903 No. 5.

2. The growth of tobacco in the Sudan except under the terms of the Proclamation of the seventeenth day of September 1900, shall be an offence under Section 1 hereof. — Growth of tobacco.

§ 2. *See the proclamation printed infra.*

3. The possession by a person of any of the articles enumerated above shall be considered as proof of his having assisted in its introduction, growth or manufacture as the case may be and shall be punished accordingly unless he can show that he obtained the same lawfully without knowing that the same was contraband. — Presumption against person in possession.

4. Offences under this Ordinance shall be tried by a Minor District Court or a Mudir's Court. — Trial of offences

5. This Ordinance may be cited as the Contraband Goods Ordinance 1901. — Short title.

The Proclamation referred to in § 2 was published in Sudan Gazette No. 16 of 1 October 1900, as follows:—

Proclamation.

Notice is hereby given that the cultivation of tobacco is entirely prohibited North of Khartoum. South of Khartoum it is permitted only with the consent of the Mudir. Such consent may be granted only in Districts where tobacco was regularly grown in the time of the Dervishes.

In connection with the above Ordinance the following Proclamations have been issued.

A.

Published in Sudan Gazette No. 60 of 1 March 1904.

Proclamation.

WHEREAS it is desirable to reinforce and amend the Proclamation dated the 17th day of September 1900 and published in the Sudan Gazette No. 16 with reference to the growth of tobacco in the Sudan.

Now it is proclaimed as follows:—

1. No person is permitted to grow tobacco in any part of the Sudan except with the leave of the Mudir.

2. This leave will only be granted to grow tobacco in places South of Wad Medani and El Obeid where it was grown in the time of the Dervishes and no greater area in such places than was cultivated then for tobacco will be allowed to be cultivated now.

3. Under no conditions whatever will tobacco be allowed to be exported to Egypt from the Sudan.

4. The import of tobacco into the Sudan is forbidden from countries other than Egypt except subject to the same duties, restrictions and conditions as would be imposed on entry into Egypt.

B.

Published in Sudan Gazette No. 64 of 1 July 1904.

PROCLAMATION.

Importation of and dealing in ammunition and explosives.

WHEREAS by the Contraband Goods Ordinance 1901 it is enacted that the importation of ammunition, gunpowder, explosives and materials for the manufacture of explosives is prohibited except under a Government permit and that the possession by a person of any of the said articles shall be considered as proof of his having assisted in its introduction, unless he can show that he obtained the same lawfully without knowing that the same was contraband. *1901 No. 13.*

It is hereby proclaimed and ordered as follows :—

1. Permits for the importation of ammunition, gunpowder, explosives and materials for the manufacture of the same will be issued only by the Agent General, Sudan Government, Cairo, to whom all applications must be made.

2. Applications for permits must state the nature and quality of the explosives which it is desired to import, and the person or company on whose behalf the application is made.

3. Every such permit shall be personal, and the explosives imported under it must not be transferred to any person not named in the permit except with the consent of the Agent General.

4. Holders of fire-arm licences and persons authorized to carry fire-arms without a licence may without a special permit import into the Sudan ammunition for their private use, made up into cartridges and suitable for the fire-arms which they are authorized to carry.

5. No private person shall except with the written consent of the Agent General or a Governor of a Province transfer whether by way of gift, sale, exchange or otherwise any ammunition to any other private person, unless such person shall be the holder of a licence or otherwise authorized to carry a fire-arm to which such ammunition is suited.

1902 No. 1.

THE SUDAN MOHAMMEDAN LAW COURTS ORDINANCE 1902.
Promulgated in Sudan Gazette No. 35 of May 1902.

An Ordinance for regulating the Sudan Mohammedan Law Courts.

Short title.

1. This Ordinance shall be called the Sudan Mohammedan Law Courts Ordinance.

Classes of Mohammedan Courts.

2. The Sudan Mohammedan Law Courts shall comprise a High Court, Mudiria and Muhafza Courts, and District Courts.

Constitution of High Court.

3. The High Court shall consist of the Grand Kadi who shall act as president, the Mufti of the Sudan, and one or more other members. The decisions of the Court shall be given by three members only.

Constitution of Mudiria and Muhafza Courts.

4. The Mudiria and Muhafza Courts shall each consist of a single Kadi. A deputy to such Kadi may be appointed when circumstances so demand.

Constitution of District Court.

5. District Courts shall each consist of a single Kadi.

Powers of Mohammedan Courts.

6. The Sudan Mohammedan Law Courts shall be competent to decide

(a) Any question regarding marriage, divorce, guardianship of minors or family relationship, provided that the marriage to which the question related was concluded in accordance with Mohammedan Law or the parties are all Mohammedans.

(b) Any question regarding wakf gift succession wills interdiction or guardianship of an interdicted or lost person, provided that the endower donor or the deceased or the interdicted or lost person is a Mohammedan.

(c) Any question other than those mentioned in the last two sections provided that all the parties, whether being Mohammedans or not, make a formal demand signed by them asking the Court to entertain the question and stating that they agree to be bound by the ruling of Mohammedan Law.

7. Questions of conflict of jurisdiction between the Civil and Mohammedan Courts shall be referred to a council consisting of the Legal Secretary of the Sudan or an official acting for him who will preside, the Grand Kadi or an official of the Mohammedan Court appointed by him, and the Judicial Commissioner or a magistrate of the Civil Court appointed by him. The decisions of this council, on questions of jurisdiction, shall be final. It shall not express any opinion on the general issues of the suit.

Conflict of jurisdiction.

8. The Grand Kadi shall from time to time, with the approval of the Governor General, make rules consistent with this Ordinance regulating the decisions, procedure, constitution, jurisdiction, and functions of the Mohammedan Law Courts and other matters connected with such Courts and the position and duties of the judges and officials of the same, and he shall with the like approval fix scales of fees chargeable in the said Courts.

Grand Kadi to make regulations.

§ 8 See Note (a).

9. The Grand Kadi or a Deputy appointed by him shall, until the Governor General otherwise directs, exercise the functions of the High Court.

Temporary composition of High Court.

§ 9 See Note (b).

10. Until the appointment of a Judicial Commissioner separate from the Legal Secretary, the third member of the council of jurisdiction mentioned in section 7 will be appointed by the Governor General.

Council of jurisdiction.

(a) *The rules made under § 8 were printed separately and in Arabic only: they have been amended by rules published in Sudan Gazette Nos. 76 and 78 of 1 May and 1 July 1905.*

(b) *In Sudan Gazette No. 61 of 1 April 1904, the following announcement was made.*

THE SUDAN MOHAMMEDAN LAW COURT.

Constitution of High Court.

His Excellency the Governor General having duly constituted the High Court of the Mohammedan Law in accordance with the Sudan Mohammedan Law Courts Ordinance the Grand Kadi will cease to exercise the functions of the High Court which were entrusted to him as a temporary measure by section 9 of the said Ordinance.

1902 No. 2.

THE SEAL ENGRAVERS ORDINANCE 1902.

Promulgated in Sudan Gazette No. 44 of February 1903.

An Ordinance for licensing seal engravers and for the registration of seals.

Licence necessary.

1. No person shall practice the trade of seal engraving without having obtained a licence from the Mudir of the Mudiria in which he resides.

Power of Mudir.

2. A Mudir shall have power :—

(1) To grant such licence as aforesaid.

(2) To delegate the power of granting such licence as aforesaid to any magistrate of the 1st and 2nd class generally in his Mudiria, or in any part thereof.

(3) To revoke such licence as aforesaid for good cause shewn.

(4) To appoint a Sheikh of seal engravers in any town he thinks fit whose duties shall be as hereinafter prescribed.

Regulations for issue of licences.

3. The following regulations shall apply to the issue of licences : —

(1) Applications shall be made by petition and accompanied by the following certificates : —

(a) A certificate from the Sheikh of seal engravers of the town or Mudiria in which the applicant resides or if there be no such Sheikh from a competent seal engraver that the applicant is skilled in such engraving.

(b) A certificate from two notables of the Mudiria in which the applicant resides that he is of their own knowledge a person of good character who has not been convicted of any penal offence mentioned in Chapters XIII, XIV, XV, XVI, XX, or XXI, of the Sudan Penal Code.

1899 No. 11.

(2) The licensing authority when granting a licence shall on payment of twenty piastres by the licensee issue to him a register book numbered on each page from one to one hundred and such register book shall bear on the front page the official seal of the licensing authority, the name of the person to whom it is issued, and the date of issue.

4. Every licensed seal engraver shall observe the following regulations :—

(a) He shall on each application for the engraving of a seal enter in the register aforesaid the following particulars :—

(1) The name in full of the applicant.

(2) The residence of the applicant.

(3) The trade or occupation of the applicant.

(4) The date of the application.

(5) Whether or not the applicant is personally known to him.

(6) The date of delivery of the seal to the applicant.

(7) A clear impression of the seal.

(b) No seal engraver shall engrave a seal for a person not personally known to him unless the applicant produces two respectable persons who will make themselves responsible for his identity and seal a certificate to that effect in the register aforesaid.

(c) No seal engraver shall engrave a seal in the name of any person other than the applicant unless the applicant produces an authority in writing from that other person witnessed by two respectable persons who will make themselves responsible that such authority was duly given and seal a certificate to that effect in the register aforesaid.

(d) Every seal engraver shall see that all entries in the register aforesaid are clearly written and without interlineation.

(e) Every seal engraver shall submit his register aforesaid for inspection to the local Sheikh of seal engravers on his demand.

(f) Every seal engraver shall on retiring from business, or on withdrawal of his licence, return all registers in his possession to the authority by whom they were issued.

(g) On the death of a seal engraver his heirs shall return all registers in the possession of the deceased to the authority by whom they were issued.

Registers returned under this sub-section may be re-issued to any licensed seal engraver succeeding to the business of the deceased.

(*h*) Every seal engraver shall engrave on all seals made by him the date of the year in which they were engraved.

Duties of Sheikh of seal engravers.

5. A Sheikh of seal engravers in relation to his duties as hereby prescribed shall be considered as a public servant and his duties shall be as follows :—

(1) He shall inspect the registers of all seal engravers under him at least once in every three months.

(2) If on inspection he finds any such register in proper and regular form he shall affix his seal and enter the date of his inspection immediately after the last entry in such register.

(3) If on inspection he finds false irregular or improper entries in any such register he shall at once take such register into his possession and send it with a report to the Mudiria in which he resides.

Penalties

1899 No. 11.

6. All offences against this Ordinance which are not punishable as offences under the Sudan Penal Code shall be punishable with a fine not exceeding £E. 1 or imprisonment not exceeding seven days or with both, and shall be triable by a Magistrate of the third class or any higher Court and summarily or otherwise.

Short title.

7. This Ordinance may be cited as the Seal Engravers Ordinance 1902.

1903 No. 1.

THE LAND ACQUISITION ORDINANCE 1903.

Promulgated in Sudan Gazette No. 45 of March 1903.
Amended by the Revision Ordinance No. 2. 1906 and printed as amended.

An Ordinance for the acquisition of land for public purposes.

Short title.

1. This Ordinance may be called the Land Acquisition Ordinance 1903.

Interpretation.

2. In this Ordinance :

The expression "land" includes benefits to arise out of land, and things attached to the earth or permanently fastened to anything attached to the earth,

The expression "person interested" includes all persons claiming an interest in compensation to be made on account of the acquisition of land under this Ordinance.

The expression " Mudir " includes any Inspector or Magistrate appointed by a Mudir to perform the functions of a Mudir under this Ordinance.

3. Whenever it appears to the Governor General that land in any locality is likely to be needed for any public purpose, a notification shall be published in the *Gazette*, and the Mudir shall publish the substance of such notification at convenient places in such locality and thereupon it shall be lawful for any person, either generally or specially authorised by the Mudir, and for his servants and workmen to do all or any of the following things, viz :— Power to make survey.

(i) To enter upon and survey and take levels of any land in the said locality ;

(ii) To dig or bore into the sub-soil ;

(iii) To do all other acts necessary to ascertain whether the land is adapted for such purpose;

(iv) To set out the boundaries of the land proposed to be taken and the intended line of the work proposed to be made thereon ;

(v) To mark such levels, boundaries and line by placing marks and cutting trenches ;

(vi) Where otherwise the survey cannot be completed the levels taken or the boundaries or line of the work marked to cut down and *clear* away any crop, fence, trees or undergrowth;

Provided that no person shall enter into any building or any enclosed court or garden attached to the dwelling house (unless with the consent of the occupier thereof) without previously giving such occupier at least seven days notice in writing of his intention to do so.

§ *3. The word in italics inserted by Revision Ordinance (No. 2) 1906.*

4. The Mudir shall at the time of such entry pay or tender payment for all damage to be done as aforesaid, and in case of dispute as to the sufficiency of the amount so paid or tendered the same shall be determined in the manner hereinafter provided for compensation on the acquisition of land. Damage done during survey.

5. Whenever the Governor General has determined to make use of the powers conferred by this Ordinance for the acquisition of Declaration of intended acquisition.

any particular land for a public purpose, a declaration signed by him shall be made to that effect.

The declaration shall contain :—

(a) A description of the land and its approximate area,

(b) If a plan has been made of such area, mention of the place where such plan may be seen.

The said declaration shall be published in the *Sudan Gazette* and shall be conclusive evidence that the land is needed for a public purpose.

Land to be marked out.

6. The Mudir shall thereupon cause the land (unless it has been already marked out under section 3) to be marked out. He shall also cause it to be measured and (if no plan has been made thereof) a plan to be made of the same.

Notices to be published.

7. The Mudir shall then cause notice of the Governor General's intention to take the land containing the particulars hereinafter mentioned to be published at convenient places on or near the said land and also to be served on the occupier and all persons believed to be interested therein or their duly authorised agents.

In case any of the persons interested resides outside the Sudan the notice may be sent to him through the post and a reasonable time allowed for reply thereto.

Such notices shall contain a sufficient description of the land and its approximate area and shall require all persons interested in the land to appear personally or by agent before the Mudir at a time and place mentioned in the notice (such time not being earlier than 14 days after publication of the notice) and to state the nature of their respective interests in the land and the particulars of their claims for compensation.

Persons interested must state names of others interested.

8. The Mudir may also require any such person to deliver him a statement of the name of every other person possessing any interest in the land or any part thereof and of the nature of such interest.

Every person required to make a statement under this or the last section shall be deemed to be legally bound to do so within the meaning of sections 141 and 142 of the Sudan Penal Code.

1899 No. 11.

Enquiry into proprietorship.

9. On the day mentioned in the notice the Mudir shall inquire into the interests of the persons interested in the land and prepare a list of the same. He shall then attempt to come to a friendly · agreement with the persons interested as to the amount of the compensation.

The Mudir may from time to time postpone the inquiry to a day to be fixed by him.

10. If the Mudir and persons interested agree as to the amount of compensation to be allowed, the same shall be expressed in an agreement signed by the Mudir and the parties interested. Agreement as to compensation.

11. If any person whom the Mudir has reason to believe to be interested does not attend, or if he is unable to agree with the persons interested as to the amount of compensation to be paid, or if any question arises of which he is unable to dispose he shall refer the matter to the arbitration of a Commission in manner hereinafter appearing. Failing agreement Commission to be appointed.

Provided that if the interests of the persons interested conflict, as in the case of landlord and tenant, then at the discretion of the Mudir or upon the demand made before the appointment of a Commission of any of the persons interested separate commissions shall be appointed for each of the parties whose interests conflict.

12. Every Commission shall consist of a President and two members. The President of the Commission shall be a magistrate appointed by the Mudir. The other two members shall be appointed as follows:— Constitution of Commission.

The Mudir shall cause a notice in writing to be served on each of the persons whom he has reason to believe to be interested in the land or who claims to be so interested requiring him at a date and place therein mentioned :—

(1) To state the compensation which he claims as compensation for his interest in the land.

(2) Jointly with the other persons interested in the land or with those of them whose interests have been referred to the same Commission to appoint a qualified person to act as arbitrator for determining the amount of compensation.

The parties interested may make such statement and appointment either verbally at the place and time mentioned in the notice or by a writing delivered to the President of the Commission previously to that date.

The Mudir shall also upon or previously to the date mentioned in the notice appoint a qualified person not being an official to act as arbitrator.

In case either of the said arbitrators are not appointed within the time aforesaid, the President of the Commission shall himself appoint an arbitrator in his stead.

Arbitrators appointed must act.

13. Every person so appointed shall be legally bound to attend and act as arbitrator unless excused for some reason to be approved by the Mudir.

Inquiry by Commission.

14. The Commission shall meet at a place and time to be fixed by the President and shall thereupon hold an inquiry and proceed to determine the amount of compensation to be paid for the interests in the land which have been referred to it and the persons to whom and the proportions in which the same is to be paid.

Mudir to furnish statement to Commission.

15. The Mudir shall furnish for the information of the Commission a statement in writing setting forth the following particulars:—

(i) The situation and extent of the land.

(ii) The names and the description of the residence and occupations of the persons whom he has reason to believe to be interested.

(iii) The amount which each of the parties interested claims as compensation for such interest.

Powers of President of Commission.

1900 No. 2.

16. In an inquiry under this Ordinance the President of the Commission shall have the same powers as to adding parties, adjournment, summoning witnesses and enforcing their attendance, examination of witnesses, and all matters of procedure as a Court under the Civil Justice Ordinance; and the procedure directed to be observed by Civil Courts shall be followed so far as it can be made applicable.

Matters to be considered in determining compensation.

17. In determining the amount of the compensation to be awarded for land acquired under this Ordinance, the following matters shall be taken into consideration:—

First.—The market value at the time of awarding compensation of such land.

Secondly.— The damage (if any) sustained by the person interested, at the time of awarding compensation, by reason of severing such land from his other land.

Thirdly.—The damage (if any) sustained by the person interested, at the time of awarding compensation, by reason of the acquisition injuriously affecting his other property whether movable or immovable in any other manner, or his earnings, and

Fourthly.—If, in consequence of the acquisition he is compelled to change his residence, the reasonable expenses (if any) incidental to such change.

Fifthly.—The increase or decrease (if any) to the value of the severed part of the land of the person interested, which is likely to accrue or be caused to it in consequence of the use to which the land acquired will be put, provided that the amount of compensation to be awarded or deducted under this head shall not exceed half of that awarded under the first head.

18. But the following matters shall not be taken into consideration:— *Matters not to be considered in determining compensation.*

First.—The degree of urgency which has led to the acquisition.

Secondly.—Any disinclination of the person interested to part with the land acquired.

Thirdly.—Any damage sustained by him which if caused by a private person would not render such person liable to a suit.

Fourthly.—Any increase to the value of the land acquired which has accrued from the publication of the intention of the Government to purchase it or to make a preliminary survey with the view of purchasing it, or which is likely to accrue from the use to which it will be put when acquired.

Fifthly.—Any outlay or improvements on such land made with the intention of enhancing the compensation to be awarded therefor under this Ordinance.

19. Every award made under this Ordinance shall be in writing signed by the President of the Commission and the other members concurring in the award and shall specify: *Contents of award.*

(1) the amount of the compensation and the persons to whom and in what proportions it is to be paid.

(2) the amount of the costs incurred in the proceedings and by what persons and in what proportions they are to be paid.

20. Every arbitrator (not being an officer of the Government) may receive such reasonable fee for his service as the Mudir shall direct. Such fee shall be deemed to be costs of the proceedings. *Arbitrator's fee*

Appeal to Civil
Court.

21. Within thirty days of the date of the award of the Commission the Government or the person interested may appeal therefrom to the principal Civil Court of the Mudiria.

If the appeal is made on behalf of the Government the Court must consist of a Civil Judge.

Procedure on
appeal.

1900 No. 2.

22. The said appeal shall be subject as far as may be to the same rules as an appeal under the Civil Justice Ordinance except as hereby otherwise provided, but the decision of the Court shall be final.

Upon the presentation of an appeal by the person interested, Court fees shall be collected upon the difference between the compensation allowed in the award and that claimed by the appellants. The appeal may be heard with assessors.

Power to take
possession after
agreement
or reference.

23. When the Mudir has made an agreement under Section 10 or a reference to a Commission he may take possession of the land which shall thereupon vest absolutely in the Government free of incumbrances.

Power to take
immediate
possession.

24. In cases of urgency when the Governor General so directs, the Mudir, although no such agreement or reference has been made may on the expiration of seven days from the publication of the notice mentioned in Section 5 take possession of any waste or arable lands needed for public purposes and such land shall thereupon vest absolutely in the Government free of incumbrances.

Standing crops
and trees.

The Mudir shall offer to the persons interested compensation for the standing crops and trees (if any) on such land; and in case such offer is not accepted the value of such crops and trees shall be allowed for in awarding compensation for the land.

Payment of
compensation.

25. Payment of the compensation shall be made by the Government according to the award or order of Court and interest at the rate of five per cent per annum shall be allowed on the amount of compensation from the date on which the Government entered into possession of the land to the date on which the compensation is paid or the Government gives notice of its readiness to pay the same.

Temporary
occupation of
land.

26. Whenever it appears to the Governor General that the temporary occupation and use of any waste or cultivated land, but not buildings, are needed for a public purpose the Mudir may be directed to procure the occupation of the same for a period not exceeding three years.

The Mudir shall then attempt to come to an agreement with the persons interested as to the amount of the compensation. If he is unable to come to an agreement he shall refer the matter to the arbitration of a Commission in like manner as is hereby provided in the case of the permanent acquisition of land.

Upon a reference being made under this section the Mudir may take possession and use the said land.

27. Upon expiration of the term the Mudir must pay to the persons interested compensation for the damage, if any, done to the land and not provided for by the award or agreement. *(Damage caused by occupation.)*

In case of dispute such compensation shall be referred to the arbitration of a Commission in the same manner as is hereby provided in the case of compensation for the acquisition of land.

Provided that if owing to the occupation the land has become unfit to be used for the purpose for which it was *used or was contemplated being used at the commencement of the said term* the Government must purchase it, if required by the parties interested, under the terms of this Ordinance.

§ *27. The words in italics inserted by Revision Ordinance No. 2. 1906.*

28. If the Governor General is satisfied that any Company or person, who is desirous of acquiring land, proposes to make use of such land for a public purpose or a purpose which is likely to prove advantageous to the Government, the Governor General may acquire such land on behalf of the Company or person in like manner as if the land was being acquired for a public purpose by the Government on behalf of itself and as a condition to such acquisition may impose such terms as to the use of such land and otherwise on the Company or person as he thinks proper. *(Acquisition of land by Governor General on behalf of companies or private person.)*

29. Service of any notice on any person interested in land to be acquired under this Ordinance may be made in the same manner and shall be subject to the same regulations as the service of summonses on defendants under the Civil Justice Ordinance. *(Service of notice. 1900 No. 2.)*

30. Whoever wilfully obstructs any person in doing any act authorised by Section 3 or Section 6 or wilfully fills up, destroys, damages, or displaces any trench or mark made under such sections shall on conviction before a magistrate be liable to imprisonment *(Penalty for obstructing survey.)*

for any term not exceeding two months or to fine not exceeding ten pounds or both.

Part only of building must not be taken.

31. The provisions of this Ordinance shall not be put into force for the purpose of acquiring a part only of any building if the owner desire that the whole of such building shall be so acquired.

1903 No. 2.

THE TAXATION OF ANIMALS ORDINANCE 1903.

Promulgated in Sud. Gaz. No. 45 of March 1903.

Short title and commencement.

1901 No. 7.

1. (*a*) This Ordinance shall be construed as one with the Taxation of Animals Ordinance 1901, and may be cited as the Taxation of Animals Ordinance 1903.

(*b*) This Ordinance shall come into force as from the 1st day of January 1903.

Amendment of Taxation of Animals Ordinance 1901.

1901 No. 7.

2. The Taxation of Animals Ordinance 1901 shall be amended as follows:— that is to say by adding in clause 4 after the last words thereof

(4) All Animals belonging to the Government or to any local public authority.

1899 No. 11

(5) Any animals belonging to officers or officials of the Egyptian or Sudan Governments or public servants as defined by the Sudan Penal Code for which forage or forage allowance is drawn from either Government or which in the opinion of the Governor General are reasonably necessary for the performance of their duties as public servants by such persons and shall by notice issued in the Sudan Gazette be declared by the Governor General to be exempt.

1903 No. 3.

THE TITLE OF LANDS ORDINANCE 1903.

Promulgated in Sudan Gazette No. 45 of March 1903.

An Ordinance to amend the Title of Lands Ordinance 1899.

Short title.

1. This Ordinance may be cited as the Title of Lands Ordinance 1903 and shall be construed as one with the Title of Lands Ordinance 1899 which with this Ordinance may be cited as the Title *1899 No. 2,* of Lands Ordinances 1899 to 1903.

2. The Title of Lands Ordinance 1899 is hereby amended as Amendment of the title of Lands Ordinance 1899. follows :—

(1) The preamble is repealed.

(2) Section 1 is repealed and in place thereof the clause fol- *1899 No. 2.* lowing is enacted: "A Land Commission shall be appointed in such provinces, districts and towns, as the Governor General may from time to time determine by notice published in the *Sudan Gazette,* to receive and adjudicate upon claims to land. Such Commission shall consist of five members selected by the Governor General of whom not less than two shall be natives of the Sudan."

(3) All words in section 2 after "as may be specified" are repealed and in place thereof the following is substituted "by notice in the *Sudan Gazette* under penalty of forfeiture."

(4) At the end of section 3 there shall be added the following :— The Commission may however upon petition presented within six months of the adjudication, order the case to be re-opened and re-hear the case. Upon such re-hearing the same fees shall be payable as upon an appeal to the Mudir under the Civil Justice Ordinance. *1900 No. 2.*

3. This Ordinance shall be retrospective and no proceeding Ordinance to be retrospective. under any Land Commission heretofore appointed shall be invalid-ated by reason of any member of such Commission not being eligible for such Commission under Section 1 of the Title of Lands Ordinance 1899 or by reason of the date fixed for the presenting *1899 No. 2.* of claims before such Commission not being fixed in the order appointing the Commission.

See the Notes and Proclamations printed with the Title of Lands Ordinance 1899. (1899 No. 2.) supra p. 10.

1903 No. 4.

THE ROYALTIES ON GUM ETC. ORDINANCE 1903.

Promulgated in the Sudan Gazette No. 46 of April 1903.

Repealed by Royalties on Gum etc. Ordinance 1904 (Sudan Gazette No. 66 of 1 September 1904) 1904 No. 7.

1903 No. 5.

THE NATIVE LIQUORS ORDINANCE 1903.
Promulgated in Sud. Gaz. No. 49 of 1 July 1903.

An Ordinance for regulating the Manufacture and Sale of Native Liquors.

IT IS HEREBY ENACTED as follows :—

Short title.

1. This Ordinance may be cited as "The Native Liquors Ordinance 1903.

Limits
of application.

2. (*a*) This Ordinance other than Part II, shall take effect throughout the Sudan.

(*b*) Part II shall take effect in such towns only as the Governor General may by notice published in the *Sudan Gazette* from time to time order.

§ *2* (*b*). *A list of the towns in which Part II has been brought into force with the numbers and dates of the Gazettes containing the notices respectively relating thereto is printed as a Schedule to this Ordinance.*

PART I.
NATIVE SPIRITUOUS LIQUORS.

No spirituous
liquors to be
manufactured in
Sudan.

3. No person shall within the Sudan manufacture any spirituous liquors nor possess or sell any spirituous liquors which have been manufactured in the Sudan under penalty of a fine not exceeding £E 10 and forfeiture of the apparatus used in the manufacture of the same.

PART II.
NATIVE ALCOHOLIC LIQUORS (NOT BEING SPIRITUOUS).

Licence
required for
manufacture or
sale of non-
spirituous
alcoholic liquors

Penalty.

4. No person shall, in any town in which this Ordinance may for the time being be in force, manufacture for sale, sell, keep for sale or offer for sale any merissa, or other native alcoholic liquor, or keep open any premises for the consumption of merissa or other native alcoholic liquor, except in virtue of a licence issued by the licensing authority, under penalty of a fine not exceeding £E. 10 and forfeiture of the apparatus used in the manufacture of the merissa or other alcoholic liquor.

5. Any person other than a person licensed under the last preceding section having in his possession, in any town in which this Ordinance may for the time being be in force, a greater quantity of merissa, or other alcoholic liquor than 30 litres shall be deemed to have the same in his possession for sale unless he proves that the same is not for sale.

6. Every licence granted under this Ordinance shall indicate the premises in respect of which it is granted and shall prescribe such conditions as to the manufacture of liquors intended for sale, hours of closing and otherwise as the licensing authority may, with the previous sanction of the Governor General, think fit.

Contents of licence.

Any breach of the conditions of the licence shall be punishable with fine not exceeding £E. 1.

Penalty.

All premises licensed under this Ordinance shall at all reasonable times be open to inspection on behalf of the licensing authority.

Inspection of premises.

7. There shall be paid for every licence under this Ordinance a licence fee at the following rates, that is to say :— For Khartoum, Omdurman and Halfaya, P. T. 25 a month ; elsewhere, P. T. 10 a month. Such licence fee shall be payable in advance on the first day of every month.

Licence fee.

8. Every licence under this Ordinance may be revoked by the licensing authority at any time.

Revocation of licence.

PART III.
GENERAL.

9. Every penalty under this Ordinance may be recovered summarily or otherwise before a magistrate of the first or second class.

Recovery of penalty.

10. The licensing authority shall be the Mudir or any first or second class magistrate appointed by the Mudir in his behalf.

Licensing authority.

SCHEDULE.

Explanation.— In the first column the names of the towns in which Part II of the above Ordinance has been brought into force are given.

The Province boundaries have been from time to time considerably altered and the names are therefore arranged under the headings of the Provinces as constituted on January 1st 1906 and not as constituted at the several dates when Part II of the Ordinance was brought into force.

The second column contains the numbers and dates of the Sudan Gazette by which Part II was brought into force in the towns mentioned in the first column.

COLUMN I. Names of towns.	COLUMN II. Numbers and dates of Gazettes.
Bahr-el-Ghazal Province—	
Wau	
Deim Zubeir	
Tonj	
Meshra-el-Rek	No. 52.
Chak Chak	1 October 1903.
Rumbek	
Shambé	
Berber Province—	
Berber	
Abu Hamed	
El-Damer	No 50.
Shendi	1 August 1903.
Metemma	
Kabushia	
Maknia	No. 76.
Sagadi	1 May 1905.
Zeidab	
Dakhila Atbara	No 78.
	1 July 1905.
Blue Nile Province—	
Wad Medani	No 51.
	1 September 1903.
Kamlin	
Eilafun	
Abu Haraz	
Helalia	
Managil	No 52.
Abud	1 October 1903.
Messellemia	
Fadassi	
Hassaheisa	
Shagal	

| Abu Deleig | } | No. 78.
1 July 1905. |

Dongola Province—

| Merowi (Tangassi)
Dongola
Kerma | } | No. 52.
1 October 1903. |

Halfa Province—

| Halfa (now known as Halfa
  Camp)
Taufikia (now known as
  Halfa)
Delgo
Kosha | } | No. 52.
1 October 1903. |

Kassala Province —

| Kassala
Gedaref | } | No. 52.
1 October 1903. |

| Gallabat | } | No. 62.
1 May 1904. |

Khartoum Province—

| Khartoum
Omdurman
Geili
Wad Ramla
Tamaniat
Wad Bishara | } | No. 50.
1 August 1903. |

Kordofan Province—

| El-Obeid
Bara
Nahud
Taiara
Um Dam | } | No. 52.
1 October 1903. |

Red Sea Province—

| Suakin
Tokar | } | No. 52.
1 October 1903. |

| Port-Sudan | | No. 77.
1 June 1905. |

Sennar Province—

| Singa | } | No. 51.
1 September 1903. |

Upper Nile Province—

    Kodok
    Taufikia   No. 52.
    Renk   1 October 1903.
    Melut

White Nile Province—

    Dueim
    Geteina
    Kawa
    Goz Abu Goma
    Hebeira   No. 52.
    Wad-el-Zaki   1 October 1903.
    Shabasha
    Garassa
    Maatuk.

1903 No. 6.

THE RUBBER ADULTERATION ORDINANCE 1903.

Promulgated in Sudan Gazette No. 49 of 1 July 1903.

An Ordinance for the detection and punishment of adulteration of India Rubber and Gutta Percha.

IT IS HEREBY ENACTED as follows :—

Interpretation

1. In this Ordinance the word "rubber" means india rubber and gutta percha in an unmanufactured state.

Rubber to be cut through centre.

2. Every ball of rubber offered for sale or exported shall be cut through the centre, and any person selling or exporting or attempting to sell or export rubber in any other condition shall be

Penalty.

punished with imprisonment which may extend to one month or with fine, or with both.

Root rubber or rubber extracted boiled bark.
Penalty.

3. Any person collecting root rubber or rubber extracted from boiled bark shall be punished with imprisonment which may extend to one month or with fine, or with both.

4. Any person who adulterates rubber by soaking in water or by mixture with sand, earth, stones, bark, leaves, wood or other foreign substance, and any person who sells or exports or attempts to sell or export rubber knowing or having reason to believe that the same is adulterated shall be punished with imprisonment which may extend to three months or with fine which may extend to £E. 10, or with both.

Adulterate d rubber.

Penalty.

5. Any rubber in respect of which any offence has been committed or is suspected to have been committed may be seized by any magistrate, police officer or official of the Custom House and may be disposed of on the conclusion of a trial in any Criminal Court under the provisions of Chapter 27 of the Code of Criminal Procedure.

Seizure of rubber.

1899 No. 12.

6. Offences under this Ordinance may be tried either summarily or not by a magistrate of the second class or any higher Court.

Trial of offences.

7. This Ordinance may be cited as "The Rubber Adulteration Ordinance 1903."

Short title.

1903 No. 7.

THE PETROLEUM ORDINANCE 1903.

Promulgated in Sudan Gazette No. 49 of 1 July 1903.
Amended by the Revision Ordinance 1906 (Sud. Gaz. No. 92 of 1 April 1906)
1906 No. 1 and printed as amended.

An Ordinance for regulating the storage of petroleum and other substances of a like nature.

IT IS HEREBY ENACTED as follows :—

1. This Ordinance may be cited as " The Petroleum Ordinance 1903," and shall come into effect on the 1st day of December, 1903.

Short title.

2. (i) No person shall store or keep any of the substances specified in the first schedule hereto except in pursuance of a licence granted by the Mudir or an officer authorized by him. The

Prohibitions.

amount of each such substance which may be kept in any one place is limited to the quantity set opposite the name of such substance in the second column of the said first schedule.

(ii) No ship or boat loaded with any such substance shall be moored nor shall land its cargo within two hundred yards of any town or village except in a berth approved by the Mudir or an officer authorized by him.

Penalty.

(iii) Any person contravening this section shall be liable to a fine not exceeding £E. 20 and to confiscation of all such materials found in his possession.

Exceptions.

3. There shall be excepted from the operation of this Ordinance:

(i) All such substances which being the property of the Government are stored or kept in any Government store or carried in any Government ship or boat.

(ii) In the case of any substance owned by private persons the amount *thereof* set opposite the name *thereof* in the third column of the said first schedule, provided that *such substance* is kept in separate glass earthenware or metal vessels each of which contains not more than 4 gallons and is securely stoppered.

§ *3. The words in italics were substituted for the original words by the Revision Ordinance 1906 (1906 No. 1).*

Issue of licence.

4. (i) Licences for the storing of such substances may be issued by the Mudir of each Province or by an officer authorized by him.

(ii) There shall be paid for each such licence the yearly sum of £E. 1.

(iii) No such licence shall be issued unless the site for the store has been approved by the Mudir.

(iv) Every roofed warehouse for the storage of such substances shall be built in accordance with the specifications set out in the second schedule hereto to the satisfaction of the Mudir.

Warehouse to be open to inspection.

5. Every such warehouse shall be at all times open to inspection by the Mudir or any officer authorized by him.

Revocation of licence.

6. Any such licence may be revoked at any time by the Mudir.

THE FIRST SCHEDULE.

List of inflammable substances.	Maximum amount which may be kept in one store.		Amount exempted.
Refined Petroleum ...	Unlimited	... ...	30 gallons.
Benzine	60 gallons...	... ...	8 gallons.
Gazolene	60 gallons...	... ...	8 gallons.
Kerosene...	Unlimited	... ...	20 gallons.
Naphthaline	60 gallons...	... ...	8 gallons.

THE SECOND SCHEDULE.

Specifications for Licensed Warehouse.

Walls to be of red brick in lime mortar not less than 50 cm. thick.

Roof to be of corrugated iron or other non-inflammable roofing material.

A separate entrance to be provided which must open direct to the air.

Floor to be sunk 15 cm. below surface of ground outside, and to be of a smooth hard surface, filled up to level of ground outside with dry sand to absorb leakage. Doorsill to be at the level of ground outside.

Good ventilation to be provided by opening at least 2 metres above ground outside : openings to be protected by wire netting of a mesh not larger than 2 cm.

1903 No. 8.

THE ARMS ORDINANCE 1903.

Promulgated in Sudan Gazette No. 49 of 1 July 1903.

An Ordinance for regulating the carrying of fire-arms.

IT IS HEREBY ENACTED as follows :—

1. This Ordinance may be cited as the "Arms Ordinance 1903" Short title and shall take effect immediately.

Repeal.
1889 No. 5.

2. The Arms Ordinance 1899 is hereby repealed.

Licence for
fire-arms.

3. (i) Subject to the exceptions hereinafter contained no person shall carry, use or have in his possession any gun, rifle or other fire-arm unless he shall be the holder of a licence for the carrying of that specific gun, rifle or other fire-arm.

(ii) Such licence may be issued by the Mudir of each Province or by an officer authorized by him, but in each case only after inquiring into the character of the applicant.

Penalties.

(iii) Any person acting in contravention of sub-section (i) shall be liable to a fine not exceeding P.T. 200 for every fire-arm carried, used or possessed by him without a licence, or to imprisonment for a term not exceeding two months and to confiscation of every such fire-arm.

Transfer of
fire-arms.

4. (i) No gun, rifle or other fire-arm shall be transferred to any person whether by way of gift, sale, exchange or otherwise, and whether such person be already the holder of a licence or not, without the written consent of the licensing authority.

(ii) Such consent may be given by any officer authorized to issue a licence to carry fire-arms in the Province in which the transfer is proposed to be made.

(iii) Such consent shall be testified by an endorsement on the licence held by the person making the transfer for carrying the fire-arm to be transferred. Such endorsement shall be signed by the officer giving such consent and the licence so endorsed shall be issued to the person to whom the fire-arm is transferred without any further charge.

Penalties.

(iv) Any person making or accepting any such transfer without such consent as aforesaid shall be liable to the penalties prescribed in section 3 hereof.

Revocation of
licence.

5. Every licence issued hereunder is subject to revocation at any time by any officer authorized to issue licenses hereunder.

Duration of
licence.

6. Every licence shall expire on the 31st day of December in each year, unless it shall be renewed by the licensing authority on that day or within 14 days thereafter.

Licence fees.

7. The following fees shall be paid on the issue or renewal of each licence :—

For each revolver   ...   P.T. 25
For every fire-arm other
   than a revolver   ...   P.T. 50

8. The Ordinance shall not apply to arms carried by any person **Exceptions.**
by virtue of his employment in the Sudan Government or Egyptian Government Services, or in any military forces stationed in
the Sudan, nor to arms carried by a commissioned officer in those
forces, or by any European officer of the Sudan Government for
his personal use, nor to arms carried by any person holding a
written exemption from the Governor General.

9. Any person holding a Licence A or a Licence B under any **Holder of**
Ordinance for the Preservation of Wild Animals for the time being **licences under Preservation of**
in force shall be entitled to have issued to him licences for two **Wild Animals**
sporting guns and three sporting rifles without paying any fee. **Ordinances.**

10. Any offence under this Ordinance may be tried summarily by **Trial of offences**
a magistrate of the first or second class. Any such magistrate
may if he think fit issue a warrant for the arrest of the offender.

11. Any police officer may seize any fire-arms carried in contra- **Powers of**
vention of this Ordinance. He shall immediately report such **police officer.**
seizure to a magistrate competent to try the offence. Failure to
produce a licence shall be *prima facie* evidence of an offence
hereunder.

1903 No. 9.

THE PRESERVATION OF WILD ANIMALS ORDINANCE 1903.

Promulgated in Sudan Gazette No. 55 (Special) December 1903.

An Ordinance for the Preservation of Wild Animals and
  Birds.

IT IS HEREBY ENACTED as follows :—

1. This Ordinance may be cited as the " Preservation of Wild **Short title and**
Animals Ordinance 1903 " and shall commence immediately. **commencement.**

2. The Preservation of Wild Animals Ordinance 1901 is hereby **Repeal.**
repealed except in so far as it repeals former Ordinances. **1901 No. 11.**

Interpretation.

3. In this Ordinance, unless there be something repugnant in the context:—

The words "Hunt," "Capture," "Kill" and "Injure" include respectively attempting or aiding to hunt, capture, kill and injure.

The words the "Licensing Officer" denote any Officer authorized by the Governor General to grant licences hereunder.

The word "notified" means notified in the *Sudan Gazette.*

The words "This Ordinance" include any regulation or matter notified or prescribed under the provisions of this Ordinance and for the time being in force.

Classification of animals and birds.

4. (1) For the purpose of this Ordinance Wild Animals and Birds are divided into four Classes, hereinafter called respectively Class 1, Class 2, Class 3 and Class 4.

(2) Class 1, Class 2 and Class 3 shall comprise the animals and birds specified in Part I, Part II, and Part III respectively of the first schedule hereto.

(3) Class 4 shall include all wild animals and birds not comprised in the said last schedule.

(4) The Governor General may at any time by notice published in the *Sudan Gazette* remove any animal or bird from any class, or include any animal or bird in any class.

Certain animals and birds absolutely protected.

5. (1) No person other than a native of the Sudan, whether the holder of a licence or not, shall kill, injure or capture any animal or bird included in Class 1.

(2) Any person killing, injuring or capturing any animal or bird in contravention of this section shall be liable to a fine not exceeding £E. 100 or to imprisonment for a period not exceeding three months.

Penalty.

Issue and provisions of licences.

6. (1) Licences for the hunting, capturing and killing of wild animals and birds included in Class 2 and Class 3 respectively may be granted by the Licensing Officer in his discretion to any person applying for the same. Such licences shall be of two kinds called respectively Licence A and Licence B.

(2) No person other than a native of the Sudan shall hunt, capture or kill any animal or bird included in Class 2 unless he is the holder of a Licence A.

(3) No person other than a native of the Sudan shall hunt, capture or kill any animal or bird included in Class 3 unless he is the holder either of a Licence A or of a Licence B.

(4) No holder of a licence shall during the currency of one licence capture or kill a greater number of animals or birds of any species included in Class 2 or Class 3 than the number specified in the first Schedule hereto opposite to the name of such species.

(5) The Governor General may at any time by notice in the *Sudan Gazette* alter the number of any species of animal or bird included in Class 2 or in Class 3 which may be captured or killed by the holder of a licence.

(6) The annual fees payable by the holders of the said licences shall be as follows :—

1. When issued to an Officer or Official of the British Egyptian or Sudan Government serving in Egypt or the Sudan or subject to approval of the Governor General to any person ordinarily resident in the Sudan or intending ordinarily to reside there.

    Licence A ... ... £E. 5
    Licence B ... ... £E. 1

2. When issued to any other person.

    Licence A ... ... £E. 40
    Licence B ... ... £E. 5

Every holder of a Licence A obtained at the £E. 5 rate shall also pay to the Licensing Officer a fee of £E. 10 for every elephant killed by him under such licence.

(7) Every Licence A and Licence B shall (except in the case of the temporary Licence B hereinafter mentioned) remain in force for one year from the date of issue and shall then expire.

(8) The acceptance of a Licence A or Licence B shall be held to constitute an agreement by the holder thereof that he agrees to conform to the provisions of this Ordinance. And no licence shall be transferable. If an original licence be lost or destroyed a duplicate licence may be obtained on proof of such loss or destruction and payment to the Licensing Officer of a fee of P.T. 25.

(9) All huntsmen, beaters and other assistants aiding the holder of a Licence A or a Licence B to hunt, capture or kill any animal or bird which such licence holder is authorized by his licence to

hunt, capture or kill shall be covered, while so acting, by such licence.

(10) Every holder of a Licence A or a Licence B shall keep an account of all animals and birds captured or killed by him of any species included in Class 2 or Class 3 and of any other species mentioned in his licence. This account shall give the date and place of capture or killing of each animal or bird captured or killed and the sex of each such animal. Every such licence holder shall produce such account together with his licence whenever called upon to do so by any Official of the Sudan Government and shall deliver a copy of such account signed by himself to the Licensing Officer upon the expiration of his licence or upon his leaving the Sudan, whichever first happens, as also, if required by the Licensing Officer for the purpose of compiling the annual returns, upon such other day as may be specified in the licence.

(11) At any time while a Licence B continues in force it may with the leave of the Licensing Officer be exchanged for a Licence A on payment of the difference between the fees chargeable for such licences respectively, but the substituted licence shall expire upon the day when the original licence would have expired.

(12) A temporary Licence B may be also granted at the discretion of the Licensing Officer for one or more days at a daily charge of P.T. 25.

(13) Any person killing, injuring or capturing any wild animal

Penalty.

or bird in contravention of sub-sections (2) or (3) or (4) of this section or refusing to produce his licence or such account as aforesaid when called upon to do so or producing an incorrect account shall be liable to a fine not exceeding £E. 100 or to imprisonment for a term not exceeding three months.

Exceptions.

7. Notwithstanding anything in this Ordinance contained the owner or occupier of any cultivated land or any person authorized by him may capture, injure or kill any wild animals or birds causing serious damage to his property if such damage cannot otherwise be averted, and notwithstanding anything in this Ordinance contained no person shall be deemed to have committed an offence under this Ordinance by reason of his having killed or injured any animal in defence of himself or any other person.

Class 4.

8. Any person may hunt, capture and kill any of the birds and animals included in Class 4.

9. (1) Licences for the hunting, capturing and killing of a specified number of animals and birds included in Class 1 may be issued in special cases to natives of the Sudan only. Each such licence shall be issued only with the approval of the Governor General, and shall be known as Licence C. The fee payable in respect of a Licence C shall be decided by the Mudir of the Province in which it is issued. *Rights of natives of the Sudan.*

(2) No native of the Sudan not being a holder of a Licence C shall hunt, kill or capture any animal or bird included in Class 1.

(3) No native of the Sudan shall employ any fire-arm in the pursuit of any animal or bird included in Class 1 or Class 2 or Class 3 whether such native shall be the holder of a Licence C or not.

(4) Subject to the above restrictions any native of the Sudan may hunt, capture and kill any wild animal or bird.

(5) Any native of the Sudan acting in contravention of subsection 2 or 3 of this section shall be liable to a fine not exceeding £E. 10 or to imprisonment for a period not exceeding three months. *Penalty.*

(6) Any native of the Sudan who is found in possession of any animal or bird included in Class 1 living or dead, or of any part of such animal or bird shall be deemed to have killed or captured such animal or bird unless the contrary be shown.

10. (1) The sale and purchase of the hides, horns or flesh or of any trophies of any of the animals and birds included in the second schedule hereto is absolutely prohibited in the Sudan. *Sale of hides, horns, etc. of certain animals prohibited.*

(2) No person shall expose or offer for sale or collect or keep for trade purposes any such hides, horns, flesh or other trophies.

(3) Any person acting in contravention of this section shall be liable to a fine not exceeding £E. 10 or to imprisonment for a period not exceeding three months, and all such hides, horns and trophies so purchased or sold, or offered for sale or collected for trade purposes shall be liable to confiscation. *Penalty.*

(4) Any person found in possession of any such hides, horns, flesh or trophies shall be deemed to have collected the same for trade purposes unless the contrary be shown.

Duty on hides, horns, etc. permitted to be sold.

11. (1) The sale and purchase of hides, horns, flesh and other trophies of wild animals and birds other than those mentioned in the second schedule hereto are permitted in the Sudan.

(2) The following *ad valorem* duties shall be paid in respect of any such hides, horns, flesh or other trophies brought into the principal town or village of any Mudiria or Mamuria for purposes of trade or exported from the Sudan :—

> On elephant or hippopotamus hides 20 per cent,
> On all other hides or skins and the flesh, horns or other trophies of any animal or bird comprised in this section 10 per cent.

(3) All such hides, flesh, horns and trophies brought into any such town or village as aforesaid shall be deemed to be brought there for the purpose of trade unless the contrary be shown.

(4) The said duty shall only be paid once in respect of each article and every official receiving payment of such duty shall if required give to the person making such payment a pass which shall authorize him to take the article in respect of which duty has been paid into any other place without paying any further duty.

(5) The holder of a licence issued hereunder shall nevertheless not be liable for the said duties in respect of the export of hides horns or other trophies obtained by him under his licence and any traveller leaving the country will be permitted to take with him free of the said duties not more than five in number of such hides, horns or other trophies upon making a declaration, if demanded, that they are not so taken for trade purposes.

(6) This section shall not apply to elephants' tusks or ostrich feathers.

Penalty.

(7) Any person failing to pay or attempting to evade the duty imposed by this section on any hides, horns, flesh or other trophies shall be liable to a fine not exceeding three times the amount of the duty and the said hides, horns, flesh and other trophies shall be liable to confiscation.

Export tax on living animals.

12. (1) From and after the date of this Ordinance an export tax according to the scale set forth in the third schedule hereto shall be levied on each living specimen of an animal or bird mentioned in the third schedule.

(2) The said export tax shall not be levied in respect of animals or birds exported by the holder of a licence issued hereunder in accordance with the terms of such licence.

(3) Any person failing to pay or attempting to evade the duty imposed by this section on any animal or bird shall be liable to a **Penalty.** fine not exceeding three times the amount of the duty and the said animal or bird shall be liable to confiscation.

13. (1) From and after the date of this Ordinance the district **Sanctuaries** bounded on the north by a line drawn from Kaka to Famaka on **for game.** the east by the Blue Nile from Famaka to the Abyssinian Frontier and then by the boundary with Abyssinia to the Baro River on the South by the Baro River to its junction with the Sobat River and then by the Sobat River to its junction with the White Nile and on the West by the White Nile shall be a sanctuary for game within which no person other than natives of the Sudan residing in the said sanctuary and Officers and Officials stationed in the same and having a special permit endorsed on their licence shall hunt, capture, or kill any wild animal or bird.

(2) From and after the date of this Ordinance the district bounded on the North by a line from Jebelein to Karkoj on the East by the Blue Nile between Karkoj and Famaka on the South by a line drawn from Famaka to Kaka and the West by the White Nile between Kaka and Jebelein shall be a reserve within which no person other than natives of the Sudan residing therein and persons having a special permit endorsed on their licences shall hunt, capture, or kill any wild animal or bird. Such special permit shall be granted at the discretion of the Licencing Officer and only to persons residing in the said District, to Officers and Officials of the Sudan Government and to Officers and Officials of the British and Egyptian Governments serving in the Sudan.

(3) The said boundary lines between Jebelein and Karkoj and between Kaka and Famaka shall be hereafter more particularly defined by a notice issued in the *Sudan Gazette.*

(4) Any person acting in contravention of this section shall be liable to a fine not exceeding £E. 100 or to imprisonment for a **Penalty.** term not exceeding three months.

14. Subject to the provisions of the last preceding section **Local extent of** every Licence A or Licence B shall be valid throughout the **licences.** Sudan save that no licence shall be valid in any part of the Sudan to which under any Ordinance of Regulations for the time being in force it is unlawful for the licence holder to proceed and that no licence shall be valid in any part of the Sudan to which special permission is required unless endorsed to that effect by the authority by which such permission is granted.

Prohibitions. Removing ostrich eggs.

15. (1) No person whether he is the holder of a licence or not shall remove or disturb or injure the eggs of an ostrich or of any other bird which may from time to time be notified without the written permission of a Licensing Officer.

Shooting from steamer.

(2) No person shall shoot from a steamer either at rest or in motion at any bird or at any animal except the lion, leopard and crocodile.

Using poison or explosive to take fish. Penalty.

(3) No person shall use any poison or dynamite or any other explosive for the taking of any fish.

(4) Any person acting in contravention of this section shall be liable to a fine not exceeding £E. 5 or in default of payment to imprisonment for a term not exceeding one month.

Special licences & dispensations for scientific purposes.

16. (1) The Governor General or any Officer authorized by him may by special endorsement on a licence permit the capture of a stated number of animals and birds included in Class 1.

(2) The Governor General may dispense from the observance of such sections of this Ordinance as he thinks proper except sub-section 1 of section 13 any person who requires such dispensation for the purpose of scientific study.

(3) Any permission or dispensation given hereunder may be withdrawn at any time.

Confiscation of small ivory.

17. All cow ivory and elephant tusks weighing less than 10 lbs, or such other weight as may be notified from time to time is liable to be confiscated and may be seized by any Magistrate, Police Officer, or Officer engaged in the Civil administration without adjudication of confiscation subject to a right of appeal to the Mudir or to a Magistrate of the 1st or 2nd Class against the confiscation.

Powers of Governor General and Governors of Provinces.

18. (1) The Governor General may from time to time by notice published in the *Sudan Gazette* exercise all or any of the following powers (that is to say):—

(a) Notify or prescribe any matter which is left by this Ordinance to be notified or prescribed.

(b) Declare a close time or close times during which any wild animal or bird specified in such notice shall not be hunted, captured or killed, nor the flesh thereof sold or offered for sale.

(*c*) Forbid or restrict the use of nets, pitfalls or other destructive modes of capture.

(*d*) Extend or limit any of the provisions of this Ordinance so as to include therein or exclude therefrom any wild animal or bird specified in such notice.

(*e*) Revoke, alter or suspend any such notices.

(2) Governors of Provinces may by public notice forbid or restrict the use within their respective provinces of nets, pitfalls or other destructive modes of capture and revoke, alter or suspend any such notice.

(3) Upon the publication of any such notice this Ordinance and such notice shall take effect as if the matter contained in such notice had been incorporated in this Ordinance.

19. Persons contravening this Ordinance by hunting, capturing or killing any wild animal or bird included in Class 2 or Class 3 without a licence or with an insufficient licence shall be liable for all the fees which would have been payable by them for the taking out of a sufficient licence for the hunting, capturing or killing of such animal or bird in addition to any fine or imprisonment which may be awarded for such contravention. *Persons contravening to pay fees as well as penalties.*

20. Prosecutions for a contravention of any of the provisions of this Ordinance may be tried by the Court of Magistrate of the 2nd Class or by any higher Court. *Trial of contraventions.*

21. The licence of any person convicted of any offence under this Ordinance shall be liable to be forfeited. *Forfeiture of licence.*

22. All animals, birds, skins, horns, tusks, feathers, trophies, eggs and carcases of all animals or birds captured or killed in contravention of this Ordinance shall be liable to confiscation and may be seized by any Magistrate, Police Officer or the Licensing Officer subject to right of appeal to the Mudir against the confiscation. *Confiscation of animals, etc.*

THE FIRST SCHEDULE.

PART I.

Class 1.—Animals and birds which may not be hunted, captured or killed:—

Giraffe	Ostrich
Rhinoceros	Shoe-bill (Balaeniceps)
Wild Ass	Ground Horn Bill (Bucorax)
Zebra	Secretary Bird (Serpentarius)

PART II.

Class 2.—Animals and birds a limited number of which may be captured or killed by the holder of an A Licence, and the number authorized of any one species:—

Mrs. Gray's Water Buck (Cobus Maria)	1	Bush Buk (Tragelaphus) ...		4
Elephant	2	Reed Buck (Cervicapra) ...		4
Eland (Taurotragus) ...	2	Jackson's Hartebeest (Bubalis Jacksoni)		4
Kudu (Strepsiceros) ...	2	Tora Hartebeest (Bubalis Tora)		4
*Hippopotamus	4	Oryx Leucoryx		6
Buffalo	4	Addax		6
Roan Antelope (Hippotragus)	4	White-eared Cob (Cobus Leucotis)		6
Oryx Beisa...	4			
Water Buck (Cubus Defassa)	4	Addra Gazelle (Gazella Ruficollis)		6

* There is no limit of the number of hippopotamus which may be captured or killed South of Kodok.

PART III.

Class 3.—Animals and birds a limited number of which may be captured or killed by the holder of an A or B Licence and the number authorised of any species :—

Ibex...	4	Ibis		...	2
Wild Sheep	4	Crowned Crane ...		...	6
Pelicans	2	†Tiang		...	12
Egrets	2	†Wart Hog		...	12
Herons	2	†Large Bustard ...		...	12
Storks	2	†Other Antelopes and Gazelles not before specified in this schedule (each species)		...	12
Marabout	2				
Spoonbills	2				
Flamingoes	2				

† A Licence holder on a trip of more than three months duration may shoot four more of each of these for food in every additional month.

THE SECOND SCHEDULE.

Animals and birds in respect of which the sale or purchase of the hides, horns or flesh or other trophies is prohibited:—

Animals and birds included in Class 1	Hartebeest
	White-eared Cob
Mrs. Gray's Water Buck	Water Buck
Kudu	Oryx
Roan Antelope	Ibex

THE THIRD SCHEDULE.

Export Tax on Living Animals:—

EACH £E. 24.

Elephant	Rhinoceros
	Giraffe

EACH £E. 10

Hippopotamus	White-eared Cob
Buffalo	Hartebeest
Wild Ass	Roan Antelope
Zebra	Oryx
Water Buck	Addax
Mrs. Gray's Water Buck	Kudu
	Eland.

EACH £E. 5

Addra Gazelle	Wild Sheep
Ibex	Balaeniceps

EACH £E. 2

Ostrich	Secretary Bird

EACH £E. 1

Lion	Leopard
	Cheetah.

1904 No. 1.

THE RAILWAY ORDINANCE 1904.

Promulgated in Sudan Gazette No. 59 of 1 February 1904.

An Ordinance for the regulation of Sudan Railways.

No. 1 of 1904.

IT IS HEREBY ENACTED as follows :—

Short title.

1. This Ordinance may be cited as the " Railway Ordinance 1904."

Application of Ordinance.

2. This Ordinance shall apply to all Sudan Government Railways and may be applied with any necessary modifications to any railway owned by private persons or companies by a notice to that effect signed by the Governor General and published in the *Sudan Gazette.* It shall not apply to any railway not used for the conveyance of passengers or goods for hire.

Meaning of " Railway."

3. Where the context so requires the word "Railway" shall include the Railway Department or the Sudan Government as owner of Railways and if applied under the Provisions of Section 2 hereof to private persons or companies shall include such private persons or companies.

Sale of goods if tolls not paid.

4. If on demand any person fail to pay the tolls due to the Railway in respect of any goods it shall be lawful for the Railway to detain and sell all or any part of such goods, or if the same shall have been removed from the premises of the Railway, to sell or detain any other goods within such premises belonging to the person liable to pay such tolls, and out of the moneys arising from such sale to retain the tolls, payable as aforesaid and all charges and expenses of such detention and sale, rendering the overplus if any, of the moneys arising from such sale, and such of the goods as shall remain unsold, to the person entitled thereto ; but no such sale shall take place until after fourteen days notice of such sale shall have been given to such person, or if he cannot be found until after fourteen days notice of sale shall have been given in the *Sudan Gazette.*

Examination of goods in case of dispute.

5. If any difference shall arise between any toll collector or other employee of the Railway and any owner of or person having the charge of any goods conveyed or to be conveyed by the Railway, respecting the weight, quantity or nature of such goods, such collector or other employee may lawfully detain such goods and examine, weigh, gauge, or otherwise measure the same ; and if upon measurement or examination such goods appear to be of greater weight or quantity or of any other nature than that stated by any person who is in charge thereof, then the owner of such goods shall be liable to pay the costs of such measurement and examination ; but if such goods appear to be of the same or less weight or quantity than, and of the same nature as, has been stated by the person in charge thereof, then the Railway shall pay such costs, and shall also pay to the respective owners of such goods, such damage, if any, as shall have arisen from such detention.

6. No person shall be entitled to carry upon the Railway or require the Railway to carry any *aqua fortis*, oil of vitriol, gunpowder, lucifer matches, or any other goods or articles which in the judgment of the Railway may be of a dangerous nature, and which may be described in any regulation of the Railway, and if any person send by the Railway any such goods without distinctly marking their nature on the outside of the package containing the same, or otherwise giving notice in writing to the book-keeper, or other employee of the Railway with whom the same are left at the time of so sending the same, he shall be liable to a fine not exceeding £E. 20 for every such offence, and in default of payment thereof, to imprisonment which may extend to six months. *Dangerous goods not to be carried without notice. Penalty.*

7. It shall be lawful for any employee of the Railway to refuse to take any parcel that he may suspect to contain any such dangerous goods or articles as aforesaid, or to require such parcel to be opened to ascertain the contents. *Dangerous goods may be refused.*

8. If any employee of the Railway shall be discharged or suspended from his office, or die, or abscond, or absent himself, and such employee or any person in whose possession is the property hereinafter specified, refuses or neglects after seven days notice in writing to that effect to deliver up to the Railway or to any person appointed by the Railway for that purpose, any station, dwelling house, office or other building with its appurtenances, or any books, papers, or other matters belonging to the Railway, which were in the possession or custody of any such employee at the occurrence of any such event as aforesaid, then, any Magistrate upon application made to him may enter or order entry to *Recovery of railway property from employees.*

be made upon such station or other building and remove or order the removal of any person found therein, and may take possession or order possession to be taken thereof, and of any such books, papers, or other matters, and shall deliver the same to the Railway or to any person appointed by the Railway to receive the same.

Railway offences.

9. Any person who does any of the things hereinafter enumerated in this section upon or relative to the Sudan Railway is guilty of a railway offence, that is to say :—

(1) Any person who travels or attempts to travel on a railway without having previously paid his fare and with intent to avoid payment thereof.

(2) Any person who refuses to show or deliver up when requested by an employee of the Railway a ticket showing that his fare is paid or to pay his fare from the place whence he started or not having produced a ticket or paid his fare, to give his name and address and a reasonable explanation of the non-production of a ticket.

(3) Any person who having paid his fare or been furnished with a pass for a certain distance knowingly and wilfully proceeds by train beyond that distance without previously paying the additional fare for the additional distance or without being furnished with a proper pass and with intent to avoid payment of such additional fare.

(4) Any person who gives in reply to a request by an employee of the Railway a false name or address.

(5) Any person who knowingly and wilfully refuses or neglects on arriving at the point to which he has paid his fare to quit any carriage.

(6) Any person who uses or attempts to use any ticket which has already been used on a previous journey.

(7) Any person who wilfully alters or defaces his ticket so as to render any writing thereon illegible.

(8) Any person who with intent to defraud uses or attempts to use any ticket on any date or for or between any stations or on any train for which the same is not available.

(9) Any person who without permission of some duly authorized employee of the Railway travels in a carriage or by a train of a superior class to that for which he has obtained a ticket.

(10) Any person found in a carriage, station or elsewhere upon the Railway premises in a state of intoxication or using obscene or offensive language or writing obscene or offensive words on any portion of the station or carriages, or committing any nuisance or otherwise wilfully interfering with the comfort of any passenger.

(11) Any person who being a passenger persists in entering a carriage or compartment of a carriage containing the full number of persons which it is constructed to convey when any person therein objects to his so entering the carriage or compartment.

(12) Any person who takes a dog or other animal into any passenger carriage.

(13) Any person who being a passenger rides on the engine or the guards van or any carriage not intended for passengers or on the roof, steps, footboard or any other part of a carriage not intended for passengers, without the permission of a railway official.

(14) Any person who being a passenger enters or leaves or attempts to enter or leave any carriage while the train is in motion or elsewhere than at the place appointed for passengers to enter or leave the carriages.

(15) Any person suffering from an infectious disorder who travels or attempts to travel or is found upon a station or station premises without the sanction first obtained of the Railway and any person who is in charge or control of or who aids or abets any person committing such offence.

(16) Any person who wilfully trespasses upon the railways, stations or other works, or is found in any carriage or building of the Railway without the permission of the Railway.

(17) Any porter, driver or conductor of any carriage vehicle or beast of burden who while in or upon any station yard or other premises of the Railway does not obey the reasonable directions of any railway employee duly authorized in that behalf.

(18) Any person who brings or places a loaded fire-arm into upon or in any railway carriage building or station or any part of any station premises.

(19) Any person who wilfully obstructs or impedes any official of the Railway in the execution of his duty.

(20) Any person committing any offence under subsection (16) hereof who refuses to quit the premises on which he is trespassing when requested so to do by any official of the Railway.

(21) Any person who wilfully obstructs any person lawfully engaged in setting out the line of a railway or who wilfully removes defaces or destroys any marks made for the purpose of so setting out the line of a railway.

(22) Any person who wilfully damages or injures the stations, carriages, or other property of the Railway or who damages or removes any part of any such property.

10. Any person who is guilty of a railway offence may be tried summarily or otherwise by a magistrate of the 1st and 2nd Class and is liable in the case of offences specified in section 8 sub-sections (1) to (17) inclusive to fine not exceeding £E. 2 and in default of payment to imprisonment not exceeding one month, and in the case of offences specified in section 8 sub-sections (18) to (22) inclusive to fine not exceeding £E. 5 and in default of payment to imprisonment not exceeding two months.

11. The recovery of the fines herein specified for railway offences shall not prejudice the right of the railway to recover any fares or damages and a magistrate may order any person convicted of any railway offence to pay any fare due or damages in respect of any injury done by him without it being necessary for the Railway to bring a civil action for the recovery of the same and any sums so ordered to be paid may be recovered in the same manner as provided for the recovery of fines under the Code of Criminal Procedure.

12. Any person committing a railway offence who refuses to give his name and address to an employee of the Railway or who has no fixed abode or who gives a name or address which appears to be a false one or who persists after warning by an employee of the Railway in committing any railway offence which causes danger annoyance or obstruction to any person may be arrested by the Police or by any employee of the Railway Company but shall be brought at once before the nearest police officer or magistrate who shall deal with the matter in the manner laid down in the Code of Criminal Procedure dealing with persons arrested without warrant.

13. Any person committing a railway offence of a continuing nature or persisting in committing any railway offence after being warned to desist by any employee of the Railway may be summarily removed by an employee of the railway from any carriage vehicle, building or other premises of the Railway.

14. Any person committing a railway offence which is also an offence under the Sudan Penal Code or any other law for the time being in force may be proceeded against alternatively under such Code or law instead of under this Ordinance and in such proceedings the provisions of section 11 hereof shall apply. Railway offences which are also offences under any other law may be dealt with under that law. *1899 No. 11.*

1904 No. 2.

THE KASSALA AND KORDOFAN TOWN LANDS ORDINANCE 1904.

Promulgated in Sudan Gazette No. 59 of 1 February 1904.
Amended by the Revision Ordinance 1906 (Sudan Gazette No. 92 of 1 April 1906).
1906 No. 1.

An Ordinance for extending the Khartoum, Berber and Dongola Town Lands Ordinance 1899 to the Towns of Kassala, Gedaref, El Dueim and El Obeid.

WHEREAS under the Khartoum, Berber and Dongola Town Lands Ordinance 1899, Commissions were appointed for those towns for the purpose of considering claims to lands and re-allotting lands with a view to the proper re-building of the said towns.

AND WHEREAS in the year 1900 a Commission was appointed for the Province of Kassala, and in the year 1903 a Commission for the Districts of El Dueim and El Obeid in the Province of Kordofan which Commissions have dealt with claims to lands in the towns of Kassala, Gedaref, El Dueim and El Obeid as if such Commissions had been appointed under the said Ordinance and the said towns included therein.

IT IS HEREBY ENACTED as follows :

1. This Ordinance may be cited as the "Kassala and Kordofan Town Lands Ordinance 1904." Short title.

2. *This Ordinance* shall be read as one with the Khartoum, Berber and Dongola Town Lands Ordinance 1899 *as amended by* To be read with Khartoum etc. Town

Lands
Ordinances
1899 No. 1.
1901 No. 1.

the Khartoum Berber and Dongola Town Lands Ordinance 1901 and shall take effect retrospectively as if it had formed part thereof.

§ *2. Words in italics inserted by the Revision Ordinance 1906 (1906 No. 1).*

Interpretation.

3. In this Ordinance the words "Town of Kassala" shall mean all that part of the old town of Kassala which was enclosed within the lines of the old fortifications, and the words "town of Gedaref," " town of El Dueim," and " town of El Obeid," all parts of those towns usually considered as such at the date of this Ordinance.

Extension of
Khartoum etc.
Town Lands
Ordinance.
1899 No. 1.

4. The Khartoum, Berber and Dongola Town Lands Ordinance 1899 *so amended as aforesaid* shall be read and construed as if the towns of Kassala, Gedaref, El Dueim and El Obeid had been named in the said Ordinance along with the towns of Khartoum, Berber and Dongola.

§ *4. Words in italics inserted by the Revision Ordinance 1906 (1906 No. 1).*

Decision
of Land
Commissions.

1899 No. 1.

5. All proceedings and decisions of any Land Commission now or hereafter taken or made in reference to lands included in the towns of Kassala, Gedaref, El Dueim and El Obeid shall take effect as if the said Commissions had been appointed under the Khartoum, Berber and Dongola Town Lands Ordinance 1899 as amended by this Ordinance.

Time for
presentation
of claims.

6. The time for the presentation of claims to land in the towns of Kassala, Gedaref, El Dueim and El Obeid shall be taken to be the respective times which have been publicly notified in that behalf in connection with the said Commissions.

Re-hearing.

7. Each Commission may upon petition presented within six months of its adjudication in any case or within three months from the publication of this Ordinance whichever is the longer order the case to be re-opened and re-hear the case.

Upon any such re-hearing after the publication of this Ordinance the same fees shall be payable as upon an appeal to the Mudir under the Civil Justice Ordinance.

Period within
which allot-
ments to be
built on.
1899 No. 1.
1901 No. 1.

8. In the application of clause 10 of the Khartoum, Berber and Dongola Town Lands Ordinance 1899 *as amended by the Khartoum, Berber and Dongola Town Lands Ordinance 1901* to the towns of Kassala, Gedaref, El Dueim and El Obeid the period of time within which the lands allotted to claimants shall be built upon

shall be the period of two years from the date of the publication of this Ordinance or from the date of the particular allotment whichever shall be the longer.

§ 8 Words in italics inserted by the Revision Ordinance 1906 (1906 No. 1).

1904 No. 3.

THE EGYPTIAN JUDGMENTS ORDINANCE 1904.

Promulgated in Sudan Gazette No. 62 of 1 May 1904.

An Ordinance for amending the Egyptian Judgments Ordinance 1901.

WHEREAS the provisions of the Egyptian Judgments Ordinance 1901 do not extend to Judgments of the Egyptian Mixed Tribunals and it is expedient in the interests of justice that such *1901 No. 4.* Ordinance should extend thereto.

NOW IT IS HEREBY ENACTED as follows:

1. This Ordinance may be cited as the "Egyptian Judgments Short title. Ordinance 1904," and shall be construed as one with the Egyptian Judgments Ordinance 1901 and may be cited therewith as the Egyptian Judgments Ordinance 1901 to 1904.

2. The Egyptian Judgments Ordinance 1901 shall be amended Amendment as follows:— of Egyptian Judgments

(a) by substituting in the preamble for the words "the Egyp- Ordinance 1901 tian Native Tribunals" the words "Egyptian Tribunals";

1901 No.4

(b) by substituting in Sections 4 and 5 for the words "Egyptian Native Court" the words "Egyptian Court, either Native or Mixed";

(c) by cancelling in Section 8 the word "native" in the phrase "Egyptian Native Tribunal" as also in the phrase "Egyptian Native Codes" at the end of the Section, and by cancelling in Section 8, sub-section (3) the words "an Egyptian local subject";

(d) by cancelling in Section 13 the word "native";

(e) by substituting in Section 14 the words "other Egyptian Tribunals" for the words "the Egyptian Native Tribunals".

1904. No. 4.

THE SUAKIN TOWN LAND REGISTRATION ORDINANCE 1904.

Promulgated in Sudan Gazette No. 63 of 1 June 1904.

An Ordinance for settling disputes as to land and for the registration of title in the town of Suakin.

WHEREAS it is expedient to establish a land register for the town of Suakin and its surroundings, and to settle all claims that may arise in connection therewith and for these purposes to appoint a Land Commission.

Short title.

1. This Ordinance may be cited as "The Suakin Town Land Registration Ordinance 1904."

Interpretation.

2. In this Ordinance unless the context otherwise requires "Suakin Town" shall include El Gaff, Quarantine Island and all lands within ten kilometres of Suakin Town. The singular shall include the plural and the masculine shall include the feminine; "Claimant" shall include a person in possession, although he does not make a formal claim; "Land" shall include buildings, trees and things attached to the land and an undivided share in land.

Appointment of Commission.

3. A Commission consisting of three members of whom one at least shall be a Notable of Suakin, shall be appointed to receive and adjudicate upon claims to land in the town of Suakin.

Presentation of claims.

4. Every person claiming to be entitled to land or to any mortgage or charge upon land or upon the produce of land in the town of Suakin shall present his claim to the Commission in writing not later than the 1st September, 1904, under penalty of forfeiture.

Adjudication and re-hearing

5. The Commission shall adjudicate upon the claim after giving such reasonable notice to the claimant and to the person in possession (if any) as shall be possible, and after hearing them or their duly authorized agents if they present themselves and save as hereinafter mentioned the decision of the Commission shall be final.

The President of the Commission may however upon petition presented within six months of the adjudication order the case to be re-opened and the Commission shall thereupon re-hear the case.

Upon such re-hearing the same fees shall be payable as upon an appeal to the Mudir under the Civil Justice Ordinance.

6. The Commission shall prepare a register upon which there Register. shall be entered the particulars of all privately owned land in the town of Suakin, and shall inscribe therein as owner the name of every claimant who is admitted to be the owner of land, whether absolutely or subject to charges and particulars of the interest of every claimant who is admitted to have an interest therein less than that of owner.

7. When the right of a claimant is admitted in respect only of Undivided an undivided share in land, and no claim to the remaining share shares. in the land is made within the time allowed by law, or such claim if made, is rejected, the claimant shall be entitled to the entirety of the land.

Nevertheless, in such case, the persons entitled to the remaining share in the land shall be allowed a further period of one year from the date of the adjudication, in which to come and claim their rights.

8. In adjudicating upon claims the following rules shall apply: Rules to be observed in
(1) Where it is shown that a person has been in possession of adjudicating. land, or in receipt of the rents or profits thereof, at each of two periods, it shall be presumed that he has been in continuous possession of the land or in continuous receipt of the rents or profits, between those periods, until the contrary be shown.

(2) No person who has been in continuous possession of land as of right or in continuous receipt of the rents and profits thereof during the five years immediately preceding the date of claim shall be required to prove the origin of his title except when there is an adverse claim by some person who has been in possession of the land or in receipt of the rents or profits thereof within the fifteen years immediately preceding the date of claim.

(3) Possession or receipt of rents or profits, by any person through whom a claimant derives his title, shall be deemed to have been possession or receipt of rents or profits, of the claimant.

(4) Where, from the relationship of the parties or from other special cause, it appears that the possessor of the land is, or was, in possession on behalf of another, his possession shall be deemed to be, or to have been, the possession of that other.

Claims on behalf of minors.

9. Where it appears to the Commission in the course of its enquiry, that a claim might be established by a minor, or by an unborn person if born, a person shall be appointed to represent the minor or unborn person, and the minor or unborn person shall be deemed to have made a claim within the time allowed by law.

Omission to present claim.

10. If the Commission be satisfied that any person who has not presented a claim is entitled to any land or to a mortgage or charge upon any land or the produce thereof the Commission may, but shall not be bound to, proceed as if he had made a claim within the time allowed by law.

Rights unenforceable except under this Ordinance.

11. No right to any interest in land which might have been made the subject of a claim under this Ordinance, shall be enforceable otherwise than in accordance with the provisions of this Ordinance.

Owners or persons in possession to mark out property.

1899 No. 13.

12. All owners or persons in possession shall before the 1st day of September 1904, mark out their property if not already sufficiently marked out, by walls, boundary stones, posts or other suitable means, and in default the Mudir of Suakin or the Commission may mark out the same at the expense of the owner, and in case of default of payment of such expense, any magistrate may upon application issue a warrant for the levy of the same in the same manner as provided in respect of a fine by the Sudan Criminal Procedure Code.

1904. No. 5.

THE TAXATION (HOUSE TAX) ORDINANCE 1904.

Promulgated in Sudan Gazette No. 66 of 1 September 1904.
Amended by the Revision Ordinance 1906 (Sud. Gaz. No. 92 of 1 April 1906)
1906 No. 1 and printed as amended.

An Ordinance for amending the Taxation (House Tax) Ordinance 1899.

Short title.

1. This Ordinance may be cited as the Taxation (House Tax) Ordinance 1904.

2. Section 4 (c) *of the Taxation (House Tax) Ordinance 1899* is hereby amended so as to read as follows:—

(c) dwelling houses and buildings in the occupation of the owner of which the annual rental does not exceed P.T. 500, provided that the same are not used as shops or factories. Amendment of Taxation (House Tax) Ordinance 1899.

§ *2. Words in italics inserted by the Revision Ordinance 1906 (1906 No. 1)*

1904 No. 6.

THE SUDAN GOVERNMENT PENSION ORDINANCE 1904.

Promulgated in Sudan Gazette No. 66 of 1 September 1904 but printed separately.

An Ordinance for authorizing and regulating the payment of pensions and gratuities to officials and others employed in the service of the Sudan Government.

IT IS HEREBY ENACTED as follows:—

CHAPTER I.
Preliminary.

1. (i) This Ordinance may be cited as the Sudan Government Pension Ordinance 1904. Short title.

(ii) It shall commence and come into effect on the first day of December 1904.

2. In this Ordinance, unless there is something repugnant in the context; Interpretation clause.

the word "official" includes any official, or other employee in the service of Government;

the word "salary" includes pay and wages;

words importing the masculine gender include females;

years, months and all other periods of time are reckoned according to the Gregorian Calendar.

3. There shall be constituted for the purposes of this Ordinance a Council consisting of the Secretary General, the Legal Secretary and the Financial Secretary to the Sudan Government. Constitution of Council.

The decision of this Council on any matter, which is referred to it by this Ordinance, shall be subject to confirmation by the Governor General, and after confirmation shall be final.

In the event of any member of the Council being absent or unable to act, his place shall be taken by such other official as the Governor General may appoint.

CHAPTER II.

To what persons pensions and gratuities are payable.

To what persons pensions and gratuities are payable.

4. (i) Except the special gratuities payable under Chapter XI of this Ordinance, the pensions and gratuities payable under this Ordinance shall be payable only to officials who have served in an established capacity in the permanent service of the Sudan Government and whom the Government has decided to permit to serve for pension or gratuity under this Ordinance, and to the widows and children of such officials.

(ii) The decision of the Government permitting any official to serve for pension or gratuity under this Ordinance will be expressed in an authority signed by the Financial Secretary, and no person shall be entitled to serve for pension or gratuity under this Ordinance, other than for such gratuities as are payable under Chapter XI, except after the issue of such an authority, nor shall any deduction towards pension under this Ordinance be made from the salary of any official except upon such an authority.

Officials excluded from pension and gratuity.

5. The following persons shall have no right to any pension or gratuity under the provisions of this Ordinance except in the special cases provided for in Chapter XI:—

(*a*) officers of the Egyptian Army serving towards pension under the Egyptian Government or in receipt of a pension from that Government;

(*b*) officials and others serving under special contracts whether with or without a right to a gratuity;

(*c*) officials and others engaged temporarily;

(*d*) officials and others, who at the date of their engagement were or are above thirty five years of age, except such officials as are exempted from this provision by virtue of section 19 of this Ordinance;

(*e*) officials while under the age of eighteen years.

6. (i) Every official must prove his age to the satisfaction of **Proof of age.** the Government by the production of a certificate of birth or other similar document before he will be accepted as serving for pension or gratuity.

(ii) In the absence of satisfactory documentary evidence as to age the Government may appoint two doctors to estimate the age of the official and the age fixed by them shall be deemed to be his age for the purposes of this Ordinance.

CHAPTER III.

Classification of officials.

7. (i) For the purposes of this Ordinance officials employed in the service of the Sudan Government are divided into two classes, namely Class A and Class B.

(ii) Class A includes every person employed in the service of **Classification** the Sudan Government whose parents were at the time of his **of officials.** birth legally domiciled in the Sudan, or in any other country lying south of the 22nd parallel of north latitude and north of the 22nd parallel of south latitude whether such person was born within or outside Sudan territory.

Explanation.—The legal domicile of any person is in general the place which is in fact his permanent home.

(iii) Class A shall also include any other person employed in the service of the Sudan Government, who, in the opinion of the Governor General, having regard to the character and climate of his native country, should fairly be so included, and who previously to any deduction towards pension having been made from such persons pay, the Governor General decides shall be so included.

(iv) Class B includes all persons employed in the service of the Sudan Government who are not included in Class A.

8. Before any official is accepted as serving towards pension, **Government's** a decision will be given as to whether he is included in Class A **decision to what** or Class B, and such decision shall be embodied in the authority **class an official** of the Financial Secretary referred to in section 4 (ii), and shall, **belongs to be** as regards such official, be final. **final.**

CHAPTER IV.

Deductions from salary towards pension.

9. (i) A deduction, which shall in no case be refunded, shall be made monthly from the salaries of all officials, who have been accepted as serving for pension or gratuity under this Ordinance. This deduction shall be made at the rate of

4 per cent for those in Class A.
5 per cent for those in Class B.

(ii) The aforesaid deduction shall not be made from the pay of any of the persons enumerated in section 5 as persons having no right to pension or gratuity under this Ordinance.

10. Except for the special gratuities payable under Chapter XI of this Ordinance, only those officials, from whose salary the aforesaid deduction had been made, shall have a right to pension or gratuity under this Ordinance.

11. Executive, travelling, climate and other allowances, gratuities and extra pay of any other kind, which may be drawn by any person employed in the service of the Government in addition to the salary of his class and category or appointment, shall not be liable to the aforesaid deduction, and shall not be taken into account in calculating the amount of any pension or gratuity.

CHAPTER V.

General rules for calculating pensions and gratuities.

12. The amount of the pension or gratuity payable under this Ordinance to any official employed in the service of the Sudan Government shall be based, subject to the regulations hereinafter contained,

(*a*) upon the amount of his salary;
(*b*) upon the length of his effective service.

13. Throughout this Ordinance the salary taken as the basis for calculating the pension of any official is the average of the salary which he has received during the last three years of his service, and every pension granted under this Ordinance shall be calculated on this basis.

Side notes:

Deduction from salary towards pension.

Only officials from whose salary deduction made have a right to pension or gratuity.

Allowances not to be liable to deduction.

Pensions and gratuities to be based on amount of salary and length of service.

Pensions are based on the average salary of last three years.

These three years must be three years of effective service, not including any periods which according to any of the provisions of this Ordinance are not to be reckoned as service towards pension. *

14. Throughout this Ordinance the salary taken as the basis for calculating the gratuity of any official is the salary drawn by him at the time of his retirement or discharge, and every gratuity payable under this Ordinance shall be calculated on this basis.

Gratuities are based on the salary at time gratuity becomes payable.

15. (i) The salary of every official, who is accepted as serving towards pension or gratuity under this Ordinance whether serving in the Sudan or Egypt, shall be fixed in respect of service in the Sudan.

Salary of officials on permanent duty in Egypt.

Whenever however such official is stationed in Egypt for permanent duty, his salary will be reduced to a rate to be fixed by the Council constituted by this Ordinance.

(ii) In computing the amount of the pension or gratuity payable to any official the calculation will be based on his Sudan rate of pay, and one fifth of the period passed in Egypt on permanent duty will be deducted from the total period of his service.

16. Effective service only is taken into consideration in calculating the period of service for pension or gratuity, leaving out of account ;

Only effective service to be counted.

(*a*) periods of leave or absence or other interruption in the service during which periods no pay has been drawn ;

(*b*) periods of sick leave during which full pay has not been drawn ;

---

* EXAMPLE.—An official receives a salary of £E. 25 monthly for one year; and a salary of £E. 30 for six months; there is then an interruption for six months of effective service on account of sick leave during which full pay is not drawn, or some other cause : he then serves at a salary of £E. 30 for two years· the average of his salary will be calculated as follows :—

30 months at £E. 30..	...	...	...	£E.	900
6 months at £E. 25...	...	...	...	£E.	150
				£E.	1,050

Average salary $\dfrac{£E. 1,050}{36}$ = £E. 29,166

(c) periods during which an official, being suspended from the performance of his duty, has forfeited the whole or a portion of his pay.

Periods of service which are excluded.

17. (i) The following periods of service also are not counted as service for pension or gratuity :—

(*a*) any period of service before the official has attained the age of eighteen ;

(*b*) one fifth of the period of service passed on permanent duty in Egypt ;

(*c*) any period of service during which the salary of an official has not been subjected to the deduction towards pension.

(ii) Officials, who are engaged provisionally with a view to their entering the permanent service of the Government, may be allowed, on their being taken into the permanent service in an established capacity, to pay the arrears of deduction for the period during which they were serving in a provisional capacity ; provided that the period for which such arrears may be paid must not exceed two years, and there must have been during it no break in the engagement; and the period for which such arrears have been so paid shall be reckoned towards pension and gratuity.

(iii) Except in the case mentioned in the last subsection and in such other cases as it is expressly permitted by this Ordinance, no payment of arrears may be made to enable a period, during which the salary of an official has not been subjected to deduction towards pension, to be reckoned towards pension or gratuity.

Addition for service south of the 12th parallel of latitude.

18. (i) An addition equal to one third of the period of service during which an official is stationed south of the 12th parallel of latitude will be made to his service in calculating the amount of his pension or gratuity. Provided that the privilege granted by this section may at any time be withdrawn as regards future periods of service by a notice published in the Sudan Gazette.

(ii) Any question arising under this section as to whether an official is stationed south of the said parallel, or as to any other matter, shall be referred to the Council constituted under this Ordinance.

19. In the case of appointments to any special office, for the due and efficient discharge of the duties of which professional or other peculiar qualifications not ordinarily acquired in the public service are required, the Governor General may by notice issued in the Sudan Gazette direct that any person so appointed may have a right to pension or gratuity under this Ordinance, notwithstanding that he is above the age of thirty five years upon appointment, and that in computing the pension or gratuity payable to any person so appointed or to his widow and children a number of years to be specified in such notice, not exceeding a maximum of ten years, shall be added to the number of years during which he may actually have served, provided that such actual service shall amount to not less than ten years or such longer period as may be named in such notice.

The aforesaid direction must be given previously to the person so appointed being accepted as serving towards pension or gratuity under this Ordinance, and the number of years to be so added shall be fixed in each case by the Council constituted under this Ordinance, subject to confirmation by the Governor General.

Professional and similar appointments.

20. In reckoning the length of an official's service for the purpose of fixing his pension or gratuity fractions of a month shall not be taken into account. A month shall be reckoned as one twelfth of a year.

Fractions of a month not counted for pension or gratuity.

21. In determining the total amount of a pension or gratuity fractions of a piastre shall not be taken into account.

Fractions of a piastre to be omitted.

22. No pension payable under this Ordinance shall in any case exceed two thirds of the average salary, determined in manner hereinbefore enacted, of the official to whom such pension is payable, nor a maximum of £E. 800.

Maximum pension.

CHAPTER VI.

Classification of pensions and gratuities.

23. Pensions and gratuities are of five kinds, namely:—

(i) pensions and gratuities upon retirement;

(ii) pensions and gratuities on account of ill health;

(iii) pensions and gratuities granted to officials on the abolition of their posts or whose services are dispensed with;

Classification of pensions and gratuities.

(iv) pensions and gratuities granted to the families of deceased officials;

(v) special pensions and gratuities granted to officials, and to the families of officials, disabled or killed by accidents arising out of and in the course of their employment.

CHAPTER VII.

Pensions and gratuities upon retirement.

Retirement on account of age.

24. (i) An official serving in Class A may be retired at any time after he has attained the age of 55 years, and, subject as hereinafter mentioned, must be retired on his attaining the age of 65 years.

(ii) An official serving in Class B may be retired at any time after he has attained the age of 50 years and, subject as hereinafter mentioned, must be retired on his attaining the age of 60 years.

(iii) Nevertheless, if any official, upon attaining the age of 65 or 60 as the case may be, is in the opinion of the Governor General engaged on service of an exceptional nature which it is considered should in the interest of the public service be completed by him before retirement, the Governor General may extend the age for his compulsory retirement for a period not exceeding five years.

Pension upon retirement.

25. (i) Officials in Class A shall have the right to a pension upon retirement at any time after the age of 55 years if they have completed twenty five years of service.

The pension of every such official will be calculated at the rate of one sixtieth of his salary for each year of service, but shall in no case exceed the maximum prescribed in section 22.

(ii) Officials in Class B shall have the right to a pension upon retirement at any time after the age of 45 years, if they have completed twenty years' service.

Officials in Class B in the service of the Government at the date of the promulgation of this Ordinance who shall not have completed twenty years' service at the age of 50 years, shall nevertheless have a right to a pension at any time after that age so soon as they have completed fifteen years' service.

The pension of every such official will be calculated at the rate of one forty eighth of his salary for each year of service, but shall in no case exceed the maximum prescribed in section 22.

26. (i) Every official in Class B, who resigns his appointment after completing seven years' service but before he is entitled to a pension, shall, upon production of such certificate as hereinafter mentioned, have the right to a gratuity of one month's pay for each years' service, but the total shall in no case exceed one years' pay. Gratuities upon voluntary resignation.

(ii) No official shall obtain a right to gratuity under this section except upon production of a certificate signed by the head official of the department in which he is serving and approved by the Governor that he has served with diligence and fidelity to the satisfaction of such head official, or if the official so resigning is the head official then upon production of a like certificate signed by the Governor General

CHAPTER VIII.

Pensions and Gratuities on account of ill health.

27. Every official, who through illness or disease contracted during his service is found under the conditions hereinafter set out medically unfit to continue in the Government service, must be retired, and shall be considered as discharged from the date of the medical certificate which finds him medically unfit to continue in the service, and the period of his service shall be calculated to the said date, provided nevertheless that if any ordinary leave is due to him he may be granted the same commencing from the date of the said medical certificate, and in that event his discharge shall date from the expiration of such leave. Retirement on account of ill health.

28. Every official retired under section 27 shall have a right to a gratuity or pension calculated as follows :— Pensions and gratuities on account of ill health.

(i) An official in Class A if he has ten years' service or less shall receive a gratuity equivalent to one month's salary for each year of service.

If he has more than ten years' service and less than fifteen years' he shall receive a gratuity calculated at the rate of one month's salary for each of the first ten years and at the rate of three month's salary for each year above ten.

If he has fifteen years' service or more he shall receive a pension equivalent to a quarter of his salary with an addition of one sixtieth of the said salary for every year above fifteen, but the total pension shall in no case exceed the maximum prescribed in section 22.

(ii) An official in Class B if he has seven years' service or less, shall receive a gratuity equivalent to one and a half months' salary for each year of service.

If he has more than seven years' service and less than twelve years, he shall receive a gratuity calculated at the rate of one and a half months' salary for each of the first seven years and at the rate of three months' salary for each year above seven.

If he has twelve years' service or more, he shall receive a pension equivalent to a quarter of his salary, with an addition of one forty-eighth of the said salary for every year above twelve, but the total pension shall in no case exceed the maximum prescribed in section 22.

Medical examination of officials claiming pension on account of ill health.

29. (i) Every official, who claims a gratuity or pension on the grounds that he is medically unfit for further service, or whom the Government calls upon to retire for the same reason, must submit himself to examination by two medical practitioners nominated by the Government.

(ii) Should one of the medical practitioners be of opinion that the state of health of the official is not such as to render him unfit for service, the official can, upon production of a certificate from a recognized medical practitioner expressing a contrary opinion, demand that his case shall be examined by a Board of referees, composed of one medical practitioner nominated by the Government, one by the official and a third nominated by the two first, the decision of which board will be final.

(iii) An official, who is not in the Sudan or Egypt at the time he claims to retire on account of ill health, must forward in support of his claim a certificate signed by two medical practitioners employed as such in the public service of the country in which he may be, and at the same time a certificate from a competent authority stating that the medical practitioners are so employed. The Government shall however in such cases have the right to require the official to submit to examination by two medical practitioners nominated by the Government, and in the event of the Government exercising such right, and the two medical practitioners disagreeing, the official shall have the same right of having his case examined by a board of referees and upon the same conditions as under subsection (ii).

CHAPTER IX.

Pensions and gratuities granted to officials on the abolition of their appointments or whose services are dispensed with.

30. An official may be retired at any time during his service in either of the following events :—

   (a) if the appointment held by him is abolished, or

   (b) if his discharge is recommended by the Council constituted by this Ordinance as being in the interest of the public service and is approved by the Governor General.

Retirement on account of abolition of appointment or on services being dispensed with.

31. Subject to the provisions of chapter XV as to the forfeiture of pensions on account of misconduct, insubordination or neglect of duty, every official discharged on one of the grounds mentioned in the last section shall have a right to a pension or a gratuity. Such pension or gratuity shall be calculated on the same scale and in the same manner as pensions and gratuities granted on account of ill health under chapter VIII.

Pensions and gratuities on such retirement.

CHAPTER X.

Pensions and gratuities granted to the families of deceased officials.

32. (i) The widow or widows of a deceased official, who at the time of his decease was in receipt of a pension, provided that the marriage was contracted three years at least before the date upon which the official retired or was discharged upon pension, and his children being issue of a marriage or of marriages contracted as aforesaid are together entitled to a pension equal to one half of the pension, of which such official was in receipt at the time of his decease.

Pensions payable to widows and children.

(ii) The widow or widows of a deceased official, who at the time of his decease was serving towards pension, provided that the marriage was contracted one year at least before his decease, and his children being issue of a marriage or of marriages contracted as aforesaid are together entitled to a pension equal to one half of such pension, if any, as he would have been entitled to if on the day of his decease he had been permitted to retire on a pension in accordance with the provisions of chapter VII, or had been discharged on a pension in accordance with the provisions of chapter IX.

(iii) The total pension granted under either of the preceding subsections shall in no case exceed £E. 200.

(iv) In the event of only one individual being entitled to the pension the proportion payable to him or her will be a quarter and not a half.

Gratuities payable to widows and children.

33. If the official at the time of his decease had less than fifteen year's service, in the case of an Official serving in Class A, and less than twelve years' service, in the case of an Official serving in Class B, his widow or widows, provided that the marriage was contracted one year at least before his decease, and his children being issue of a marriage or marriages contracted as aforesaid are together entitled to half the gratuity to which he would have been entitled if he had, on the day of his decease, been discharged under the conditions of chapter IX.

Division of pensions and gratuities amongst widows and children.

34. (i) A pension or gratuity granted to the family of a deceased Mohammedan official shall be divided amongst the members of his family having a right to a share under the provisions of this Ordinance in accordance with Mohammedan Law ; that is to say, any share, which under Mohammedan Law would have gone to any member of the family who has no right to a share under this Ordinance, shall accrue to the members of the family having a right to share under this Ordinance in the same relative proportions as they take in their original shares.

(ii) In the case of Officials who are not Mohammedans the pension or gratuity granted to their families shall be divided in the following shares :

To the widow one half if there are children, and the whole if there are no children, but in the latter case in accordance with section 32 (iv) the amount of the pension but not of the gratuity is reduced :

To the children, who are given a right to share under the provisions of this Ordinance, one half in equal shares if there is a widow and the whole in equal shares if there is no widow.

35. The following members of a family are not entitled to a share in a pension or gratuity :— Members of family who are excluded from pension.

    (*a*) the sons of officials who are 18 years of age and upwards at the date of the officials' decease ;

    (*b*) daughters who are married at the date of the officials' decease ;

    (*c*) daughters who are 20 years of age and upwards at the date of the officials' decease.

36. The divorced wife of an official has no right to pension or to gratuity. Divorced wife excluded.

37. The following forfeit their right to pension and will cease to draw it :— Forfeiture of pensions of widows and children.

    (*a*) widows who remarry ;

    (*b*) sons so soon as they attain the age of 18 years ;

    (*c*) sons who are employed in any capacity by the Sudan or Egyptian Governments, or who are educated at the expense of the Sudan or Egyptian Governments, or who are sent abroad at the expense of either Government to complete their education : provided however that their rights to pension shall be re-established if they are discharged from Government employment or leave a school for any reason other than misconduct ;

    (*d*) daughters who marry ;

    (*e*) daughters so soon as they attain the age of twenty.

38. Widows, who remarry and afterwards are divorced or again become widows, shall not thereby re-establish their right to pension. Widows and daughters who forfeit pension on marriage cannot subsequently re-establish right to it.
Similarly daughters, who have married, if they are afterwards divorced or become widows, shall not thereby re-establish their right to pension.

39. The pension or share of a pension of a widow or a child which is forfeited under section 37 is not transferable to any other members of the family and ceases to be payable. Share of a widow or child does not accrue on her on his death to the others.

CHAPTER XI.

Special pensions and gratuities granted to officials, and to the families of officials, disabled or killed by accidents arising out of and in the course of their employment.

When and to
whom granted.

40. (i) Special pensions or gratuities will be granted to :—

(*a*) officials who as the result of an accident arising out of and in the course of their employment are disabled so as to be no longer capable of continuing in the Government service ;

(*b*) the widows and children of officials who have been killed by an accident arising out of and in the course of their employment or have died from the result of an accident so arising.

Provided that the injuries are not attributable to the wilful misconduct or neglect of the officials in question.

(ii) The provisions of this chapter shall apply also to temporary officials and employees, to officials and employees engaged under contract when their contract contains no clause entitling them or their families to compensation, pension or gratuity in case of death or disablement, and to all unpensionable employees.

It shall not apply to officials of the Egyptian Government pensionable under Egyptian Law who have not elected to come under this Ordinance, nor to officers of the Egyptian Army so pensionable, nor to non-commissioned officers and men of the Egyptian Army who have a right to compensation under Egyptian Law.

How calculated
in case of
officials who
have contrib-
uted towards
pension.

41. Officials from whose pay the deduction towards pension has been made, and who are disabled in manner aforesaid, shall have their right to a pension calculated in the following manner.

An official, whether in Class A or Class B, if at the time of the accident he has less than seven years' service, which may be reckoned service towards pension, shall receive a pension equivalent to a quarter of his salary.

If he has seven years' service and less than twelve, he shall receive a pension equivalent to one third of his salary.

And if he has twelve years' service and less than twenty five years' service in the case of an official in Class A, or than twenty years' in the case of an official in Class B, he shall receive a pension equivalent to five twelfths of his salary.

And if he has twenty five years' service in the case of an official in Class A, or twenty years' service in the case of an official in Class B, or more, he shall receive the pension which he would have received upon being retired at the time of the accident without any restriction as to age.

But the pension in none of these cases shall exceed the maximum prescribed in section 22.

42. Widows and children of an official, who has been killed in the performance of his duties or who has died in manner aforesaid, shall receive a pension equal to half the pension which the official himself would have received under the provisions of the preceding section.

How calculated in case of widows and children of officials who have contributed towards pension

43. Temporary and unpensionable officials, who are disabled in manner aforesaid, shall receive a gratuity equivalent to one month's salary for each year's service for the first ten years of their service and to two months' salary for each year's service above ten.

The gratuity however shall in no case be less than £E. 20 or more than £E. 400.

How calculated in the case of temporary officials.

44. The widows and children of a temporary or unpensionable official, who has been killed or has died in manner aforesaid, shall receive a gratuity equal to half the gratuity which the official would have received under the provision of the preceding section.

How calculated in the case of widows and children of temporary officials.

45. The provisions of chapter X as to the division amongst widows and children of their pensions and gratuities, the circumstances under which widows and children have no right to pension or gratuity, and the circumstances in which widows and children lose their rights to pension, and otherwise regulating the pensions and gratuities of widows and children shall apply to the pensions and gratuities granted to widows and children under this chapter of the Ordinance; except that the provision that the marriage must have been contracted one year at least before the official's decease shall not apply.

Provisions as to pensions and gratuities granted to widows and children.

46. (i) In all cases of accident to an official arising or alleged to have arisen out of and in the course of his employment, and resulting in death or disablement, the deceased or disabled official will be medically examined as soon as possible after the accident.

Medical examination and enquiry as to the accident.

The examination will be held by two medical practitioners in the service of the Government, who will report whether or not in their opinion the official has been killed or disabled as the result of an accident incurred in the performance of his duties, and in case of disablement, whether such disablement is likely to be permanent or temporary, and will give the reasons for their opinion.

If two medical practitioners in the service of the Government cannot be obtained, the examination and report may be made by one such medical practitioner; but the report must contain a statement of the reasons which make this necessary; and the Government may in such case require a second report to be made by two other medical practitioners.

(ii) An enquiry will also be held by a board of two or more officials, nominated for the purpose by the Head of the Department in which the deceased or disabled official was serving or by the principal Government official at the place of the accident, to ascertain whether the accident to the official arose out of and in the course of his employment and whether it was attributable to his wilful misconduct or neglect; and the evidence taken upon such enquiry, and the conclusion of the official or board who hold the enquiry, shall be embodied in a written report.

(iii) The reports of the medical practitioners and that made on the above mentioned enquiry shall be forwarded to the Financial Secretary.

When special pensions granted to disabled officials become definite.

47. The special pensions granted to disabled officials shall not become definite until the Government is satisfied that the disability is permanent. Until the Government is so satisfied the disabled official must submit himself to medical examination whenever required by the Financial Secretary.

CHAPTER XII.

Special provisions as to officials in the service of the Government previously to this ordinance, and as to officials transferred from or to other Governments.

Government to decide whether existing officials will be permit-

48. As soon after the promulgation of this Ordinance as may be, the Government will decide, in the case of every official employed in the service of the Government at the date of the promulgation of this Ordinance, whether he shall be permitted to contribute towards pension and gratuity, and every such decision shall be embodied in an authority signed by the Financial Secretary, and must be accepted by the official within six months of being communicated to him or it will be cancelled.

ted to serve for pension.

49. (i) Every official employed in the service of the Sudan Government at the date of the promulgation of this Ordinance, who is accepted as serving towards pension or gratuity, shall have the right to have his back service under the Sudan Government taken into account in calculating his pension or gratuity, subject to the payment by him to the Financial Secretary of the arrears of the deduction towards pension in respect of such back service.

Back service of existing officials who are permitted to serve for pension.

(ii) The period of such back service shall be calculated in accordance with the rules as to service contained in chapter V.

(iii) The amount of such arrears and the period of back service shall be stated in the aforesaid authority of the Financial Secretary, and such statement shall be conclusive as regards the said official.

(iv) The amount of the said arrears may be paid by equal monthly instalments spread over a period not exceeding that for which they are due.

(v) In the event of the death or retirement of the official before the whole amount of the said arrears has been paid up, the period of service, in respect of which the said arrears have not been paid up will not be taken into account in calculating his pension or gratuity, unless he or his next of kin or representatives at once pay up the balance of the said arrears.

50. (i) Every official of the Egyptian Government pensionable under Egyptian Law, who has been or shall be permanently transferred to the Sudan Government and whose claims towards pension or gratuity have not been settled by the Egyptian Government, may be granted the right to come under this Ordinance upon condition of releasing his claim under Egyptian Law.

Officials of Egyptian Government permanently transferred to Sudan Government may be permitted to come under this Ordinance.

(ii) Any such official, who is serving with the Sudan Government upon the promulgation of this Ordinance and elects to come under the same, shall not be entitled under Section 25 to a Pension upon voluntary retirement, unless in addition to satisfying the conditions of Section 25 he completes five years service with the Sudan Government from the promulgation of this Ordinance.

(iii) In calculating the period of service for pension or gratuity of any such official, who elects to come under this Ordinance within six months from the promulgation thereof, his service towards pension under the Egyptian Government previously to his so electing shall be reckoned as follows.

(a) Periods of service in the Sudan or on the Red Sea Littoral shall be reckoned in accordance with the Khedivial Pension Decree under which the official was serving.

(b) Periods of service in Egypt shall be decreased by one fifth.

(c) The allowance made by Egyptian Law for war service shall be counted.

(iv) In the case of any such official, who is granted the right to elect to come under this Ordinance at any time after six months from its promulgation, his service towards pension under the Egyptian Government previously to his so electing shall be reckoned in manner directed by the last subsection, except that the Council constituted under this Ordinance shall have the power to make such reduction of the allowance made to him by the Khedivial Pension Decree for his service in the Sudan or on the Red Sea Littoral as having regard to the higher rate of pension allowed under this Ordinance they consider fair.

Officials of the Sudan Government transferred to the Egyptian Government.

51. In the event of an official being transferred with the consent of the Governor General to the service of the Egyptian Government, and of the Egyptian Government permitting his service under the Sudan Government to be reckoned towards the pension or gratuity payable to him by the Egyptian Government, the Sudan Government shall contribute such proportion of the pension or gratuity, if any, which ultimately becomes payable to him as may be agreed upon between the two Governments.

Pensions and gratuities payable to officials transferred from another service under the British Crown.

52. (i) An official, who has been transferred to the service of the Sudan Government from another service under the British Crown, shall upon retiring have a right to pension for the period of his service under the Sudan Government, provided that the total period of service towards pension under the Sudan Government and the British Crown together shall be of such a length as, if he had served the whole under the Sudan Government, would have entitled him, upon retiring under the like circumstances, to a pension under this Ordinance. Such an official shall nevertheless not be entitled under Section 25 to a pension upon voluntary retirement unless he completes such a period of service with the Sudan Government as shall have been fixed in his case by the Council constituted under this Ordinance.

(ii) In like manner, such an official shall upon retiring have a right to a gratuity for the period of his service under the Sudan Government, provided that the total period of his service towards pension under the Sudan Government and the British Crown together shall be of such a length as, if he had served the whole under the Sudan Government, would have entitled him, upon retiring under the like circumstances, to a gratuity under this Ordinance.

53. (i) An official, who before he has obtained a right to pension upon retirement under chapter VII is transferred with the consent of the Governor General to another service under the British Crown, shall upon retiring from that service have a right to a pension for the period of his service under the Sudan Government, provided that the total period of his service towards pension under the Sudan Government and the British Crown together shall be of such a length as, if he had served the whole under the Sudan Government, would have entitled him, under the like circumstances, to a pension under this Ordinance.

Pensions and gratuities payable to officials transferred to another service under the British Crown or Egyptian Government.

(ii) In like manner, such an official shall, upon retiring from the service of the British Crown, have a right to a gratuity for the period of his service under the Sudan Government, provided that the total period of his service towards pension or gratuity under the Sudan Government and the British Crown together shall be of such a length as, if he had served the whole under the Sudan Government, would have entitled him, upon retiring under the like circumstances, to a gratuity under this Ordinance.

54. (i) The pensions granted under sections 52 and 53 shall be based upon the average salary drawn by the official during the last three years of his service under the Sudan Government, and shall be calculated for an official in Class A at the rate of one sixtieth of such average salary for every year of his service under the Sudan Government, and for an official in Class B at the rate of one forty-eighth of such average salary for every year of his service under the Sudan Government; except that special

Calculations of such pensions and gratuities.

pensions granted under chapter XI to officials transferred to the Sudan Government shall be calculated at the rates laid down in that chapter, no account being taken of service other than that under the Sudan Government.

The said pensions shall in no case exceed the maximum prescribed in section 22.

(ii) The gratuities granted under sections 52 and 53 shall be based on the salary drawn by the official at the time of his retirement or discharge from the Sudan Government and shall be calculated in respect of his period of service under the Sudan Government at the same rate for every year of service as they would be calculated under this Ordinance if the whole of the service spent by him under the Sudan Government and the British Crown had been spent under the Sudan Government.

Pensions and gratuities payable to the widows and children of an official transferred from or to another service.
55. The widow or widows and children of an official transferred to or from the Sudan Government service under the conditions stated in sections 52 and 53 shall upon his decease have a right to a share of the pension, of which such official was in receipt at the time of his decease, or of the pension or gratuity, to which he would have been entitled if on the day of his decease he had been permitted to retire on a pension in accordance with the provisions of chapter IX; and the provisions of chapter X shall apply to the pension or gratuity payable to such widows or children.

CHAPTER XIII.

Claims to Pensions and Gratuities.

Claims to be examined by Financial Secretary.
56. No official shall be discharged or permitted to retire under conditions which would entitle him to a pension or gratuity under this Ordinance, until his claim has been enquired into and approved by the Financial Secretary.

Period within which claim must be made.
57. (i) Every claim for payment of a pension or gratuity must be made within six months of the date upon which the official ceased to draw his salary or died.

(ii) Every claim not presented within the period prescribed in the preceding clause shall be disallowed, and the claimant shall lose all rights to pension or gratuity, unless he proves that it was impossible for him to make his claim within such period.

58. Every claim to a pension or gratuity must be addressed to the Financial Secretary either direct or through the Head of the Department or Governor of the Province in whose budget the pay of the official was provided.

All claims to be addressed to the Financial Secretary.

59. (i) Every claim for pension or gratuity made by the widows or children of a deceased official or pensioner must be accompanied by a certificate of the death of the official or pensioner together with a declaration in the form set out in Appendix A, signed by the claimant and certified by a competent authority.

Documentary evidence required upon claims by widows or children.

(ii) In addition, a certificate in the form set out in Appendix A, signed by two officials of the Government who are still serving or who have retired upon pension, must be furnished that the particulars set out in the said declaration are true, and as to the dates of the marriages of the deceased.

(iii) If the claimant is residing outside Egypt or the Sudan there may be furnished in lieu of the said certificate a declaration to the same effect, sworn before a commissioner of oaths, notary public, magistrate or other official authorized to attest sworn statements, by some person who was well acquainted with the deceased and not related to him or his widow, and accompanied by official copies of the certificate of marriage of the deceased and of the births of his children.

(iv) Whoever in any declaration or certificate required by this Section makes any statement which is false and which he either knows or believes to be false or does not believe to be true touching any material point, shall be liable to the punishment enacted in the Sudan Penal Code for persons who give false evidence.

1899 No. 11.

60. Any objection to the amount or assessment of a pension or gratuity, whether on the part of the Government or the person entitled to the pension or gratuity must be made within four months from the date that the amount of the pension or gratuity as approved by the Financial Secretary has been notified to the person so entitled or if the person so entitled is residing outside Egypt and the Sudan then within six months from the date of such notification. After that date the amount or assessment of a pension or gratuity shall not be subject to question and no action shall lie on account of any error in such amount or assessment.

Date after which amount or assessment of a pension or gratuity shall not be subject to question.

CHAPTER XIV.

Payment of Pensions.

Date from
which pensions
are payable.

61. The date from which a pension becomes payable to an official is the day following that on which he has ceased to draw the salary for his services, and in the case of widows and children the date of the decease of the official.

Manner of
payment.

62. Pensions are paid by equal monthly instalments in arrear by the Financial Secretary's Department and by Governors of Provinces when authorized to pay them by the Financial Secretary. Under no circumstances shall any payment in advance be made.

Payment of part
of pension or
gratuity
pending its
determination.

63. (i) Pending the determination of the exact amount of the pension to which an official or other person is entitled, the Financial Secretary may authorize the payment of a part, not exceeding one half, of the pension to which the official or other person appears to be entitled, provided that the official or other person to whom the pension is to be paid signs a declaration in the form set out in Appendix B.

(ii) Under the same conditions a part, not exceeding one half, of any gratuity may be paid pending the determination of the exact amount.

Commutation of
pensions.

64. The Government shall have the right to commute any pension payable under this Ordinance in accordance with actuarial tables, which may be issued for this purpose from time to time with the approval of the Council constituted under this Ordinance.

Pensions and
gratuities are
inalienable.

65. Subject as hereinafter mentioned pensions and gratuities are not subject to deductions and are inalienable and not liable to be taken in execution or other legal process.

They are however subject to deduction not exceeding in all one quarter of the total pension or gratuity

(*a*) to defray debts incurred by the official to the Government;

(*b*) to pay maintenance, alimony or other family allowances ordered to be paid by a court of competent authority.

CHAPTER XV.

Forfeiture of rights to pension and gratuity.

66. (i) Any official, who

(*a*) upon conviction for any offence is sentenced to death or imprisonment without the option of a fine, or

(*b*) is dismissed for misconduct, insubordination or neglect of duty, from the service of the Sudan Government or of any other Government to which he has been transferred under the provisions of chapter XII, shall be liable to forfeit all rights to pension or to gratuity, even although such gratuity has been liquidated or such pension is actually being paid.

(ii) The case of every such official shall be considered by the Council constituted under this Ordinance, who shall have power to forfeit his rights to pension or gratuity either wholly or in part from the date of his sentence or dismissal and their decision subject to confirmation by the Governor General shall be final.

(iii) If any official after a decision wholly forfeiting his rights to pension or gratuity is permitted to re-enter the service, his previous service shall not be reckoned towards pension or gratuity.

Forfeiture upon sentence of death or imprisonment or dismissal for misconduct.

67. An official who resigns forfeits all rights to pension or gratuity, except such pension or gratuity, if any, as is payable to him upon resignation in accordance with the provisions of chapter VII.

Forfeiture upon resignation.

68. Any official, who having retired on a pension under this Ordinance and having subsequently been permitted to re-enter the permanent service in an established capacity continues to draw his pension at the same time as his salary, will be dismissed and will forfeit all rights to pension.

Forfeiture of pension of official who draws salary and pension at same time.

69. Pensions of which the arrears have not been drawn for three years from the date of the last payment, and gratuities which have not been drawn within two years of the date upon which they become due cease to be payable and are annulled, unless the claimant proves that it was impossible for him to claim the same within that period.

Annulment of unclaimed pensions and gratuities.

70. All arrears of pensions which are not claimed within one year of their becoming due are forfeited, unless the claimant proves that it was impossible for him to claim the same within that period.

Forfeiture of unclaimed arrears of pensions.

CHAPTER XVI.

Re-engagement of pensioners.

Pensions of pensioners re-entering the service to be suspended and reassessed.

71. (i) When an official, having retired and being in receipt of a pension under this Ordinance, is readmitted to the Government service, whether in a temporary or permanent capacity, the payment of his pension shall be suspended.

At the conclusion of his services when he again retires the payment of his pension shall be resumed.

(ii) A pensioner thus re-engaged in a permanent and established capacity shall have the right, when he again retires or is discharged, to have his pension reassessed, and to reckon as service towards pension any period or periods of permanent service subsequent to the date when he was first placed upon pension, provided that such service has been of such a nature as may under the provisions of this Ordinance be reckoned as service towards pension.

Upon reassessment of pension or gratuity former service to be counted subject to repayment of former gratuity if any.

72. (i) Every official, who having quitted the Government service after contributing towards pension under this Ordinance, is subsequently permitted to re-enter it in a permanent and established capacity, shall have the right, except in those cases mentioned in section 66 to reckon his former service towards the pension to which he will eventually be entitled, provided that such former service could have been so reckoned before he quitted the service.

(ii) But if such official has received a gratuity on leaving the service, he shall have the option on re-entry, either to retain the gratuity, in which case his former service shall not be reckoned towards the pension to which he may eventually be entitled, or to refund the gratuity within one year of the date of his re-entry into the service and to reckon his former service towards pension.

(iii) In the case of the death or retirement of the official before the whole amount due has been refunded, then, in calculating what pension or gratuity is eventually due to him or to his widows and children, the period of service, in respect of which the amount of a gratuity not refunded was paid, will not be taken into account, unless such amount is paid without delay by him or by his next of kin or representative.

73. An official who has retired from the service with a pension or gratuity under this Ordinance on account of ill health or of injuries received shall not be readmitted to the service, unless he is certified by two medical practitioners nominated by the Government to be fit for further service.

Officials retired for ill health or disablement not to be re-engaged except on medical certificate.

APPENDIX "A."

Claim for a pension or gratuity on behalf of the family of

....

I.................................the undersigned request that a pension or gratuity shall be awarded to the family of

....

late official, employee, or pensioner of the Government, and declare that the said family consists of the persons named below and of such persons only, and that none of the said widows were divorced nor have married again, and none of the said daughters have married, and that the particulars given with respect to the said family are true.

WIDOW OR WIDOWS.	SONS.		DAUGHTERS.	
Name.	Name.	Age.	Name.	Age.

Place..............................

....

Signature

Date..............................

CERTIFICATE.

We the undersigned having known the deceased, declare that to the best of our belief the above particulars of the members of the family of the late ....are correct in all respects. We certify that the marriage of the deceased with...was celebrated on...........................

Place................................

....

Date ....

....

Signatures

APPENDIX "B."

The Sudan Government having consented to award to me provisionally a pension (gratuity) of L.E........................ .. ..a month pending the carrying out of the enquiries necessary for the exact determination of the pension (gratuity) due to me, I hereby declare that I acknowledge that the pension (gratuity) now awarded to me is subject to revision, and should the sum now paid to me be greater than the sum to which I shall eventually be found to be entitled, I undertake to refund any excess in the amount now paid to me.

....
Signature.

Place.................................

Date.................................

1904 No. 7.

THE ROYALTIES ON GUM ETC. ORDINANCE 1904.

Promulgated in Sudan Gazette No. 66 of 1 September 1904.
Amended by the Revision Ordinance 1906 (Sudan Gazette No. 92 of 1 April 1906)
1906 No. 1 and printed as amended.

An Ordinance for regulating the royalties on Gum, Ostrich
Feathers, Rhinoceros Horn, Ivory, India Rubber and Gutta
Percha.

IT IS HEREBY ENACTED as follows:

1. This Ordinance may be cited as "The Royalties on Gum etc.   Short title.
Ordinance 1904."

2. The following Ordinances are hereby repealed:—   Repeals.

   (i) The Royalties on Gum etc. Ordinance 1899.   *1899 No. 4.*

   (ii) The Royalty on Gum etc. Ordinance 1901.   *1901 No. 2.*

   (iii) The Royalties on Gum etc. Ordinance 1903.   *1903 No. 4.*

3. The Notices and Proclamations in respect of the collection   Withdrawal of
of royalties issued in Sudan Gazette Nos. 20, 29, 33, 34, 43, 44, 54   Notices and
and 64 respectively are hereby withdrawn.   Proclamations.

§ *3. Words in italics added by the Revision Ordinance 1906 (1906 No. 1).*

4. Royalties shall be levied on all Gum, Ostrich feathers, Ivory,   Upon what
Rhinoceros horns, India Rubber and Gutta Percha coming from   goods and at
any part of the Sudan or imported into the same in an unmanu-   what rate
factured condition at such rate as shall from time to time be   royalty to be
notified by the Governor General in the Sudan Gazette not   levied.
exceeding a maximum of 20 °/$_o$ or a minimum of 10 °/$_o$ ad valorem.

Until further notice the royalty on Gum, Ostrich feathers, India
Rubber and Gutta Percha shall be 20 °/$_o$ ad valorem and the
royalty on Ivory and Rhinoceros horn shall be 15 °/$_o$ ad valorem.

5. For the purpose of ascertaining the amount of royalty   Valuation
payable in each case tables showing the valuation for purposes of   tables.
royalty of each of the goods above mentioned shall be published
from time to time and the royalty shall be calculated from the
valuation table for the time being in force. The valuation table
contained in the Schedule hereto shall be and remain in force
until further notice. It shall be lawful for the Governor General

to make any alteration in classification or valuation by notice published in the Sudan Gazette.

At what places royalties payable.

6. All goods liable to royalty must be taken to the prescribed weighing station and must not be taken away until the royalty has been paid and a pass for such goods has been granted.

Provided always that passes may be granted at weighing stations authorizing payment at some other place named therein and in such case the royalty shall be paid accordingly.

The prescribed weighing stations shall be as mentioned in the second part of the Schedule hereto, but the Governor General may from time to time alter the same by notice published in the Sudan Gazette.

Payment to be in cash.

7. All royalties must be paid in cash.

Packages to be stamped.

8. Packages containing goods in respect of which the royalty has been paid shall be marked with a Government stamp. No goods liable to payment of royalty under this Ordinance shall be exported from the Sudan except in packages bearing the Government stamp.

Trading in ivory rubber or gutta percha south of Khartoum.

9. (1) No person may trade in or purchase Ivory India Rubber or Gutta Percha south of Khartoum unless he is the holder of a Government Licence or permit authorizing him to do so. The Government may refuse any such licence or permit.

(2) The holder of any such licence or permit must conform to the conditions endorsed upon it under penalty of revocation of the same and confiscation of all Ivory Rubber or Gutta Percha in his possession.

Penalty.

(3) Any person trading in or purchasing Ivory Rubber or Gutta Percha in contravention of Sub-section (1) shall be liable to a fine not exceeding L.E. 100.

(4) Offences under sub-section (1) may be tried by a Magistrate of the first or second class.

Upon contravention goods may be seized.

10. All goods liable to royalty in respect of which the provisions of this Ordinance are contravened may be seized by any Magistrate or Police Officer and may be confiscated by any Magistrate of the first or second class.

THE SCHEDULE.

PART I.

Table of Valuation for the purpose of calculating Royalties.
This table was repealed by the notice printed infra.

PART II.

Stations for payment of royalty.

The prescribed weighing station for all goods consigned to Omdurman or Khartoum is at Khartoum North. For all other goods the prescribed weighing station is the nearest weighing station to the place of collection provided that if such weighing station is not on the trade route for such goods, they may be taken instead by the direct road to the nearest weighing station to such route.

Under § 5 of the above Ordinance the following notice has been published by order of the Governor General.

Promulgated in Sudan Gazette No. 81 of 1 Sept. 1905.

THE ROYALTIES ON GUM ETC. ORDINANCE 1904.

In accordance with Section 5 of the Royalties on Gum etc. Ordinance 1904 the table of valuation contained in the Schedule thereto is repealed as and from the dates hereunder specified and in lieu thereof the following table shall come into force as regards Ivory from the 1st October 1905 and as regards the other articles mentioned therein from 15th September 1905 :—

Table of Valuation for the purpose of calculating Royalties.

1. Gum :—

    Hashab ... ... P.T. 65 *per kantar.*
    Gezira ... ... „ 50 „ „
    Talh ... ... „ 40 „ „

2. Ostrich Feathers :—

    White ... ... P.T. 100 *per rotl.*
    Black ... ... „ 40 „ „
    Rabda ... . „ 25 „ „

Table of Valuation for the purpose of calculating Royalties.
(continued).

3. Ivory :—

1st Quality "Aal"	...	...	...	£E. 40 *per kantar.*
2nd Quality "Mashruk"		...	...	„ 32 „ „
3rd Quality "Bar"	...	...	...	„ 25 „ „
4th Quality "Masbrukh Mashmus"	...		„ 15 „ „
5th Quality "Khorda" ...	...	...	„ 10 „ „

4. Rhinoceros Horn :—

1st Quality	...	...	...	... P.T. 15 per rotl.
2nd Quality	...	...	...	... „ 10 „
3rd Quality	...	...	...	... „ 5 „

5. India Rubber and Gutta Percha :—

All Qualities   ...   . £E. 10 per kantar.

NOTE.—*The words in italics were added by the Notice published in Sudan Gazette No. 103 of December 1906.*

1905 No. 1.

THE MAGISTERIAL AND POLICE POWERS ORDINANCE 1905.

Promulgated in Sudan Gazette No. 73 of 1 March 1905.

An Ordinance for authorizing the Conferring of Magisterial powers on public servants and for granting magisterial and Police powers to Officers and Men of the Slavery Repression Department.

WHEREAS by section 23, sub-section 1, of the Sudan Code of Criminal Procedure the Governor General is empowered to confer on any military officer serving or employed in the Sudan and qualified to sit on Courts-Martial all or any of the powers of a magistrate of the first, second or third class.

1899 No. 12.

And whereas it is desired to authorize the appointment as magistrates of other public servants.

And whereas it is also desired to grant certain magisterial and police powers to Officers and Men of the Slavery Repression

Department of the Egyptian Government while serving in the Sudan.

IT IS HEREBY ENACTED as follows :—

1. This Ordinance may be cited as " The Magisterial and Police Powers Ordinance 1905."

Short title.

2. The Governor General may confer on any public servant of the Sudan Government and on any public servant of the Egyptian Government when employed in the Sudan, whether such public servant is a military officer or not, all or any of the powers of a magistrate of the first, second or third class under the Criminal Procedure Code.

Power of Governor General to confer magisterial powers on public servants.

1899 No. 12.

3. By virtue of his office an Inspector of the Slavery Repression Department while serving in the Sudan shall be a magistrate of the second class under the Criminal Procedure Code.

Slavery Inspectors to be second class magistrates
1899 No. 12.

4. Non-commissioned officers and men of the Slavery Repression Department shall have the like powers of arresting and such other powers as are conferred on Police officers by the Criminal Procedure Code.

Men of Slavery Department to have Police Powers.
1899 No. 12.

5. The Governor General shall have power to confer on any commissioned or non-commissioned officer of the Slavery Repression Department the powers of a Police Officer in charge of a Police Station under the Sudan Criminal Procedure Code.

Power of Governor General to confer Powers of Police Officer in charge of Police Station.
1899 No. 12.

1905 No. 2·

THE LOST AND UNCLAIMED PROPERTY ORDINANCE 1905.

Promulgated in Sudan Gazette No. 73 of 1 March 1905.
Amended by the Revision Ordinance (No. 2) 1906 (Sud. Gaz. No.　of
1906 No.　and printed as amended.

An ordinance as to the disposal of lost or unclaimed property in the posesssion of the Police, the Sudan Government Railways, and the Department of Steamers and Boats.

IT IS HEREBY ENACTED as follows :—

1. This Ordinance may be cited as " The Lost and Unclaimed Property Ordinance 1905."

Short title.

Register of Lost and Unclaimed Property to be kept at the Offices of Mamurs.

2. A register shall be kept at every Mamur's Office of all lost or unclaimed property which has been found by or handed to the Police or other official, and a list of all such property shall be posted in a conspicuous place outside the Mamur's Office.

Sale.

3. If such property is not claimed within twenty-one days' time in the case of an animal, or within one year in the case of other property, it may be sold by public auction and the proceeds credited to the Government. Perishable property may be sold at the discretion of the Governor of the Province or an inspector within a shorter period.

Finder's remuneration.

4. Any person who finds and hands any lost property, other than a live animal, to the police shall be entitled by way of remuneration to a tenth of its value or of the proceeds of its sale. *If the owner thereof reclaims such property he shall pay this remuneration in accordance with the valuation of the property to be made by a Magistrate as well as any expenses incurred in respect of the same.*

§ 4. *The sentence in italics was substituted by the Revision Ordinance No. 2 1906 (1906 No.   ) for the original sentence.*

Disposal of Proceeds of Sale.

5. The owner of the property shall be entitled to receive the proceeds of the sale, less any expenses incurred by the authorities and any finder's remuneration, upon application made within two years of the property having come into the possession of the authorities. After that period the proceeds of sale shall be *the property of* the Government.

§ 5. *The words in italics were substituted for the original words by the Revision Ordinance (No. 2) 1906 (1906 No.   ).*

Registers to be kept by the Sudan Government Railways and by the Steamers and Boats Department.

6. A similar register or registers shall be kept by the Sudan Government Railways and by the Department of Steamers & Boats of all lost or unclaimed property in their possession found in any train, vessel, station, quay, enclosure or premises belonging to the said Railways or Department.

Disposal of property by the Sudan Government Railways and by the Steamers and Boats Department.

7. Any lost or unclaimed property, and also any property in the possession of the said Railways or said Department of which the owner or consignee cannot be found, or of which in the case of animals or perishable property the owner or consignee fails to take delivery within seven days of receiving notice of the arrival of the same, may be sold and the proceeds credited to the said Railways or said Department after the following period:—

(a) In the case of perishable goods, after such period as the authorities of the said Railways or said Department (having regard to the condition of the said goods) may determine.

(*b*) In the case of animals, after a period of ten days from the receipt of the said notice, and

(*c*) In the case of other property, after a period of six months from its coming into possession of the said Railways or said Department or from its being ready for delivery to the consignee as the case may be. '

Provided that the owners of animals or of perishable property sold shall be entitled to receive the proceeds of sale, less the expenses incurred, upon application made within six months from the date of such animals or property having come into the possession of the said Railways or Department.

8. The owner reclaiming any such property as is mentioned in the last section shall be bound to repay to the said Railways or Department the expenses (if any) incurred in the custody and care of the same. Owner to repay expenses of custody.

1905 No. 3.

THE AUCTIONEERS', BROKERS' AND PEDLARS' ORDINANCE 1905.

Promulgated in Sudan Gazette No. 73 of 1 March 1905.

An Ordinance for regulating and licensing the occupation of Auctioneer, Market Broker and Pedlar.

IT IS HEREBY ENACTED as under :—

1. This Ordinance may be cited as "The Auctioneers', Brokers' and Pedlars' Ordinance 1905." Short title.

2. The Licence (Auctioneers and Pedlars') Ordinance, 1899 is hereby repealed, but this repeal shall not affect any licences already duly issued thereunder. Repeal.
1899 No. 10.

3. In this Ordinance a "Pedlar" shall mean any person who travels from place to place or market to market or goes to other men's houses and carries to sell or exposes for sale any goods or exposes for sale samples of goods to be afterwards delivered, but Definitions.

it shall not include any person who sells only vegetables, fruit, cereals, flesh, fish, or other victuals the produce of the Sudan, or articles of local manufacture made by himself or any member of his family.

Auctioneers, Simsars and Pedlars to be licensed.

4. No person shall act as an auctioneer, simsar or market broker or trade as a pedlar except by virtue of a licence to be issued after inquiry as to the character of the applicant by the Governor or other officer authorized by him.

Period of Licence.

5. Every such licence shall expire on the 31st day of December in each year, but no penalty shall be incurred if the licence is renewed on or before the following 14th day of January.

Fees payable on Licences.

6. (i) The annual fee for an auctioneer's, simsar's or market broker's licence shall be P.T. 100.

(ii) The annual fee for a pedlar's licence shall be P.T. 50.

(iii) For a licence taken out on or after the 1st day of July in any year only half the fee shall be paid.

Penalties

7. (i) Every person acting as an auctioneer, simsar or market broker without a licence shall be liable to fine not exceeding P.T. 50 in respect of each occasion on which he so acts.

(ii) Every person trading as a pedlar without a licence shall be liable to fine not exceeding P.T. 50 for every week or part of a week during which he so trades.

Regulations by Governors.

8. (i) A Governor may issue regulations for auctioneers, simsars, market brokers and pedlars, which shall be approved by the Governor General and endorsed on licences.

Penalties for breach of regulations.

(ii) Breach of such regulations may be punished by revocation of licence and the infliction of such fines not exceeding P.T. 100 as may be specified in such regulations.

By what Courts offences triable.

9. Offences under this Ordinance may be tried summarily or otherwise by any magistrate of the first, or second class but no revocation shall be effective unless passed or confirmed by the Governor.

1905 No. 4.

THE TAXATION (HOUSE TAX) ORDINANCE 1905.

Promulgated in Sudan Gazette No. 73 of 1 March 1905.

An Ordinance for Amending the Taxation (House Tax) Ordinance 1899.

IT IS HEREBY ENACTED as follows :

1. This Ordinance may be cited as "The Taxation (House Tax) Ordinance 1905." *Short title.*

2. Sections 3 and 5 of the Taxation (House Tax) Ordinance 1899 are hereby repealed. *Repeal. 1899 No. 7.*

3. Section 3 is hereby re-enacted as follows:— *House Tax payable by owner quarterly in arrear.*

The tax shall be payable in arrear by four equal instalments on the 31st day of March, the 30th day of June, the 30th day of September and the 31st day of December in each year.

The tax shall be payable by the owner of the premises assessed, who shall be liable for every instalment of tax unpaid, whether he was or was not the owner at the time the instalment became due.

4. Premises shall not be liable to house tax for any portion of a year they are unoccupied. Provided that premises shall not be exempt under this section unless they have been unoccupied for one month of 30 continuous days. Premises which have been unoccupied for a continuous period exceeding 30 days shall, be exempt for the whole of such period. Provided further that the notices described in section 6 of this Ordinance have been duly given. *Premises unoccupied for 30 days exempt.*

5. In the event of any question arising as to whether the premises are or have been in fact occupied or unoccupied the same shall be decided by a magistrate of the first or second class. *Question as to occupation of premises by whom decided.*

The owner of the premises may appeal within one calendar month from a decision. Such appeal shall be heard by the Civil Judge, if located in the Province, or, if a civil judge is not located in the Province, the appeal shall be heard by the Governor or a magistrate of the first class nominated by him for the purpose.

Notice of Premises becoming unoccupied or re-occupied to be given to the Mamur.

6. The owner of the premises shall give notices to the Mamur stating that the premises are unoccupied or have become re-occupied and the date upon which they became unoccupied or re-occupied. The notices shall be delivered within 7 days after the premises have been vacated or become re-occupied. If a notice that premises have been vacated is not given within 7 days after their becoming vacated the premises shall, for the purpose of house tax, be considered to be occupied until such notice is given, and if notice that premises have become re-occupied is not given within 7 days of their becoming re-occupied the premises shall be liable to double house tax from the time of their becoming re-occupied until such notice is given.

1905 No. 5.

THE PREVENTION OF CRUELTY TO ANIMALS ORDINANCE 1905.

Promulgated in Sudan Gazette No. 80 of 24 August 1905.

An Ordinance for Preventing Cruelty to Animals.

IT IS HEREBY ENACTED as follows :—

Short title.

1. This Ordinance may be cited as "The Prevention of Cruelty to Animals Ordinance 1905."

Application of Ordinance 1899 No. 11.

2. This Ordinance shall apply to those parts of the Sudan only in which the Sudan Penal Code is for the time being in force.

Definition of "Animal."

3. In this Ordinance the word "Animal" means any domestic animal or any wild animal in captivity and includes birds.

Definition of "Cruelty."

4. In this Ordinance every person is said to be guilty of cruelty to animals who commits or abets the commission of any of the following offences that is to say who

(1) Overloads any animal,

(2) Employs any animal which by reason of sickness wounds or infirmity is not in a fit condition to work,

(3) Neglects any animal in such a manner as to cause it unnecessary suffering.

(4) Wantonly and without sufficient cause illtreats any animal,

(5) Engages in promotes or organizes cock fighting or other combats between animals.

5. Whoever is guilty of cruelty to animals shall be punished with a fine not exceeding £E. 5 or with imprisonment not exceeding one month or with both.

Punishment for Cruelty.

6. No criminal proceedings in respect of offences under this Ordinance shall be taken after the expiration of one month from the commission of the offence.

Time limit within which proceedings must be taken.

7. Offences under this Ordinance may be tried by the Court of a 3rd class magistrate or any higher Court and summarily or otherwise.

Jurisdiction.

8. On conviction of an offence under this Ordinance a Magistrate may in addition to or in substitution for any penalty under this Ordinance make an order for the temporary custody by the Police Authorities of an animal the subject of the offence and may order the person convicted to pay such a sum meanwhile as the Magistrate thinks fit for the maintenance of such animal and such sum shall be recoverable in the same manner as a fine inflicted under the Sudan Penal Code.

Custody of Animal.

1899 No. 11.

9. A Magistrate shall have power where a conviction has been obtained in the case of an animal suffering from incurable disease or injury to order such animal to be destroyed.

Destruction of Animal.

1905 No. 6.
THE LAND SETTLEMENT ORDINANCE 1905.

Promulgated in Sudan Gazette No. 80 of 24 August 1905.
Amended by the Revision Ordinance (No. 2) 1906. (Sudan Gazette No.   of   )
1906, No.   and printed as amended.

An Ordinance for the settlement of rights over waste forest and unoccupied lands and to provide for the expropriation of such rights.

WHEREAS it is expedient to make special provision for the settlement of claims to waste forest and unoccupied lands.

IT IS HEREBY ENACTED as follows :—

1. This Ordinance may be called "The Land Settlement Ordinance 1905."

Short title

Definitions
" Land."

2. In this Ordinance the word "land" includes benefits to arise out of land and things attached to the earth or permanently fastened to anything attached to the earth.

" Unoccupied Land."

The words "unoccupied land" include uncultivated land and all land which shall not have been in the uninterrupted occupation of some person or persons for a period exceeding five years next before a notice given by the Governor General with reference to such lands under the next section and also all lands which owing to their height above the river the infrequency of rains and other circumstances have been cultivated at irregular intervals only.

Notice to be given of proposed settlement of unoccupied lands and of appointment of settlement officer.

3. (i) Whenever it shall appear expedient to the Governor General to effect a settlement of claims in or over any lands which are or are alleged to be waste forest or unoccupied h : shall publish a notice in the Sudan Gazette

(a) specifying as nearly as possible the situation and limits of such land,

(b) declaring it is proposed to effect a settlement of such land,

(c) appointing an Officer (hereinafter called the Settlement Officer) to enquire into and determine the existence nature and *extent of any* rights claimed by or alleged to exist in favour of any personin or overany land comprised within such limits and to deal with the same as provided in this Ordinance.

(ii) The Governor General may at any time by a notice in the Sudan Gazette annul the appointment of any Settlement Officer or appoint another Officer in his place.

§ *3.* (i) (*c*) *Words in italics inserted by the Revision Ordinance (No. 2) 1906 (1906 No.   ).*

Proclamation by Settlement Officer.

4. When a notice has been published under section 3 the Settlement Officer shall publish in Arabic at the offices of the Governor of the Province and the Mamur of the district and at convenient places in the neighbourhood of such land a proclamation

(a) specifying as nearly as possible the situation and limits of the land which it is proposed to settle,

(b) fixing a period within which any person claiming any right in or over such land is required to present to such Officer a written notice specifying the nature of such claim.

5. (i) After the expiration of the period specified in section 4 the Settlement Officer shall hold enquiries at convenient places on or near the land which it is proposed to settle. Such reasonable notice as may be possible of the date and place of such enquiries shall be given to the claimants. Enquiry by Settlement Officer.

The Settlement Officer shall enquire into all claims made under section 4 and the existence of any right or practice in or over the land in respect of which no claim has been made and shall record a summary of his enquiry in writing.

(ii) And after hearing the claimants or their duly authorized agents if they present themselves the Settlement Officer shall adjudicate upon every claim.

6. (i) If the Settlement Officer is satisfied that any person is entitled to the beneficial ownership of any land he shall make an order admitting such ownership. Settlement Officer to decide as to ownership and as to rights not amounting to ownership.

(ii) If the Settlement Officer is satisfied, as regards any land, that it is entirely free from any private rights or that the rights existing in or over it do not amount to full ownership he shall make an order that the ownership of the land is in the Government.

(iii) If the Settlement Officer is satisfied, that any person is entitled to any rights of the kind mentioned hereinafter in or over any land owned by the Government or any other person, or that the Government is entitled to any such right of a private nature in or over land owned by any person, that is to say

(*a*) a right to cultivate by the natural flood of the river or by rain,

(*b*) a right of pasture,

(*c*) a right to forest produce,

(*d*) any other beneficial rights or practice, the Settlement Officer shall make an order admitting the rights and defining the same.

(iv) The Settlement Officer may but it shall not be necessary for him to record

(*a*) a right of way,

(*b*) a right to a watercourse or to the use of water.

(v) Where a claim to any right is admitted the Settlement Officer shall record the local limits within which such right may be exercised the extent to which the benefit thereof may be leased sold or bartered and such other particulars as may be necessary to define the nature incidents and extent of the right.

Rules to be
followed in
adjudicating
upon Claims.

1899 No. 2.
1905 No. 5.

7. In adjudicating upon claims to land the following rules shall be followed : —

(i) The rules laid down for land commissions by the Title of Lands Ordinances shall be followed by the Settlement Officer, so far as they are not inconsistent with this Ordinance; provided that a claimant shall not be barred under section 10 of the Title of Land Ordinance 1899 on account of his not having presented a claim under that Ordinance, if he has during the five years preceding the presentation of his claim to the Settlement Officer exercised as of right any beneficial right in or over the land in question.

(ii) All waste forest and unoccupied land shall be deemed to be the property of the Government until the contrary be proved.

(iii) In the case of land which under the customary methods in use with regard to the same is cultivable at irregular intervals, the fact that a person has cultivated the same for whatever period shall not by itself give him the absolute ownership of the land.

(iv) The exercise by any person of rights in or over one or more portions or parcels of land shall not be taken as a presumption in his favour as against the Government of ownership of any rights in or over any greater extent of land than that in or over which such rights were exercised.

Presumption
that rights
are in gross and
inheritable.

8. All rights admitted by the Settlement Officer and recorded in his order shall be presumed to be in gross and inheritable unless it is otherwise stated in the order.

Rights
enforceable
only under this
Ordinance.

9. No right in or over any land which might have been made the subject of a claim under this Ordinance other than a right of way or to a watercourse or the use of water shall be enforceable otherwise than in accordance with the provisions of this Ordinance.

Powers of
Settlement
Officer holding
an enquiry.

10. In an enquiry under this Ordinance the Settlement Officer shall have the same powers as to summoning witnesses, and compelling their attendance, and administering oaths, and as to all matters of procedure as a Court under the Civil Justice Ordinance, and the procedure directed to be observed by Civil Courts shall be followed so far as applicable.

Power to
expropriate
private rights.

11. Whenever a scheme or a provisional scheme has been approved for the artificial irrigation of any land which has been or

may be declared to be Government land under this Ordinance or such land is needed for building or for a public purpose the Governor General may compulsorily expropriate all private rights, if any, existing in or over such land.

12. Whenever the Governor General has determined to make use of the powers conferred by the last section in respect of any particular land, a notice signed by him, containing a declaration to that effect, shall be published in the Sudan Gazette. Such notice may be added to the notice published under section 3 or may be a separate notice. Notice to be given of proposed expropriation.

It shall be conclusive evidence that the land is needed for a purpose authorized by this Ordinance.

13. The Settlement Officer shall thereupon proceed to expropriate all rights existing in or over such land in manner provided by the Land Acquisition Ordinance 1903 as hereinafter varied. Settlement Officer to effect expropriation. *1903 No. 1.*

14. For the purpose of such expropriation Procedure on expropriation. *1903 No. 1.*

(i) The Settlement Officer shall be deemed to be a Governor proceeding under the Land Acquisition Ordinance 1903.

(ii) The claimant shall be deemed to be a person interested and appearing before him in pursuance of a notice given under section 7 of that Act, and the provisions of the preceding sections shall be deemed to have been complied with.

(iii) In the event of the Settlement Officer failing to come to a friendly agreement with the persons interested under section 9 the matter shall be settled by him as sole arbitrator and for that purpose he shall have the powers of and be subject to the like provisions as a Commission of Arbitration appointed under Section 12 of the Land Acquisition Ordinance 1903.

(iv) The Settlement Officer may award compensation in land or partly in land and partly in money.

(v) If the compensation consists of land and the Government shall not be ready to give delivery of the same to the persons interested simultaneously with the taking over by the Government of rights expropriated from them the Settlement Officer shall award compensation by way of rent from the date when the Government enters into possession of such rights to the date when the Government delivers the land or notifies its willingness to do so.

(vi) In determining the amount of compensation for rights which have no market value or of which the market value does not represent the full value to the person interested the arbitrator shall take into consideration in addition to the other matters mentioned in section 17 of the Land Acquisition Ordinance 1903 the profit derivable by the persons interested from the exercise of such rights. If the arbitrator shall award compensation in land the land shall be of such area and so selected that it shall be as profitable to the person interested as the rights expropriated from him.

1903 No. 1.

(vii) If upon the expropriation of rights over "karu" or "bugr" lands artificially irrigated land is awarded by way of compensation the land so awarded shall not be less in area than one tenth of the "karu" or "bugr" lands over which such expropriated rights extend.

Provided that upon the recommendation of the Settlement Officer the Governor General may dispense with this rule in particular cases where such compensation would be in the opinion of the Settlement Officer undoubtedly excessive.

Appeals.

15. (i.) An appeal shall lie from any order made by a Settlement Officer under section 6 or 14 of this Ordinance to such civil judge or magistrate of the first class as the Governor General may appoint to hear appeals from such orders.

(ii) Every appeal under the last foregoing section must be presented within six months of the order. It shall be made by petition in writing and may be delivered to the Settlement Officer who shall forward it without delay to the Officer competent to hear the same.

(iii) Every such appeal shall be heard in the manner prescribed for the hearing of appeals by the Court of the Mudir under the Civil Justice Ordinance and the same fees shall be payable in respect thereof as on an appeal to the Court of the Mudir under that Ordinance and the order passed on such appeal shall be final.

Restraint on alienation.

16. Any rights over land declared to be Government land under this Ordinance and any land granted by way of compensation under this Ordinance shall not be alienated or mortgaged or charged except with the consent of the Governor of the Province and any alienation or mortgage or charge or attempt to alienate mortgage or charge without such consent shall be void.

Such consent shall not however be required to a lease of such rights or land for a period not exceeding three years or to their devise by will.

17. A Settlement Officer may from time to time with the previous consent of the Governor of the Province stop any public or private way or watercourse. *Power to stop ways and watercourses.*

Provided that for the way or watercourse so stopped another way or watercourse which in the opinion of the Governor is equally convenient already exists or has been provided or constructed by the Settlement Officer.

1905 No. 7.

THE VAGABONDS ORDINANCE 1905.

Promulgated in Sudan Gazette No. 80 of 24 August 1905.

An Ordinance for more effectually dealing with idle persons and vagabonds.

IT IS HEREBY ENACTED as follows:—

1. This Ordinance may be cited as "The Vagabonds Ordinance 1905." *Short title.*

2. In this Ordinance *Definitions of "idle person."*

(i) the term "idle person" shall include :—

(*a*) Any person who being able wholly or in part to maintain himself or his family wilfully neglects or refuses to do so,

(*b*) Any person who wanders abroad or places himself in any street or public place to beg or gather alms or causes or encourages children to do so unless from age or infirmity he is unable to earn his living and

(*c*) Any person who has no settled home and has no ostensible means of subsistence and cannot give a satisfactory account of himself.

Explanation.— In order to convict a person under sub-clause (*c*) all the things therein mentioned must be proved. A Nomad Arab cannot be convicted because he has no settled home if he has either apparent means of subsistence or gives a satisfactory account of himself.

"Vagabond." (ii) The term "vagabond" shall include :—

(*a*) Any person who after being convicted as an idle person commits any of the offences which would render him liable to be convicted as such again,

(*b*) Any person who is found in possession of house-breaking implements with intent to commit any of the offences defined in Sections 353 to 357 inclusive of the Sudan Penal Code,

1899 No. 11.

(*c*) Any suspected person or reputed thief who by night frequents or loiters about any shop warehouse dwelling house dock or wharf with intent to commit any offence under Chapter XIX or XX of the Sudan Penal Code.

1899 No. 11.

(*d*) Any male person who knowingly lives wholly or in part on the earnings of a prostitute or in any public place solicits or importunes for immoral purposes and

(*e*) Any male person who dresses or is attired in the fashion of a woman in a public place or who practices sodomy as a means of livelihood or as a profession.

"Incorrigible vagabond." (iii) An "incorrigible vagabond" shall mean any person who after being convicted as a vagabond commits any of the offences which would render him liable to be convicted as such again.

Penalty on conviction as idle person. **3.** Whoever is convicted as being an idle person shall be punished with imprisonment for a term which may extend to one month or with fine or with both.

Penalty on conviction as vagabond. **4.** Whoever is convicted as being a vagabond shall be punished with imprisonment which may extend to three months or with fine or with both.

Penalty on conviction as incorrigible vagabond. **5.** Whoever shall be convicted as being an incorrigible vagabond shall be punished with imprisonment which may extend to one year or with fine or with both.

Security for good behaviour. **6.** On the conviction of any person as an idle person or as a vagabond the Court shall have power in addition or in substitution for any other punishment to order the prisoner to enter into a bond with one good surety in such a sum as the Court shall think fit that he will be of good behaviour for a period not exceeding one year and in default of his finding such a surety the Court shall have power to order him to be imprisoned in lieu thereof until the period for which he was ordered to give such security expires or until he gives the security to the Court requiring it in addition to any other punishment which may be adjudged to him.

7. Whenever the Court is of opinion that any person imprisoned for failing to give security under this Ordinance whether by the order of the Magistrate of such Court or that of his predecessor or of some subordinate Magistrate may be released without hazard to the community or to any other person he may order such person to be discharged.

Court may release person imprisoned for failure to give security.

8. Whenever any person has been imprisoned for failing to give security under this Ordinance the Court or any superior Court may make an order reducing the amount of the security or the time for which the security has been required.

Court may vary order as to security.

9. Offences under this Ordinance may be tried by any magistrate of the second class or any superior Criminal Court and summarily or otherwise.

Jurisdiction.

10. In proving the intent to commit an offence under the Sudan Penal Code it shall not be necessary to show that the person suspected was guilty of any particular act tending to show this purpose or intent and he may be convicted if from the circumstances of the case and from his known character as proved to the Court before which he is brought it appears to the Court that his intent was to commit such offence.

Evidence of intent to commit an offence.

1899 No. 11.

ILLUSTRATION.

A man who has been convicted of theft is found by night crouching in the shadow of a locked shop and seeing a policeman at once runs away. He is arrested in possession of a large bundle of keys. It need not be shown that he was trying the keys or attempting to enter the shop.

1905 No. 8.

THE ANTIQUITIES ORDINANCE 1905.

Promulgated in Sudan Gazette No. 80 of 24 August 1905.

Amended by the Revision Ordinance (No. 2) 1906 (Sud. Gaz. No.   of 1906 No.   and printed as amended.

An Ordinance for making provision for the better preservation of antiquities in the Sudan.

IT IS HEREBY ENACTED as follows :—

Short title.

1. This Ordinance may be cited as "The Antiquities Ordinance 1905."

Definitions
" Antiquities."

2. (i) In this Ordinance

"Antiquities" mean all buildings monuments remains or objects of whatever age or people which are illustrative of art science industry history religion literature or custom and were built produced or made in the Sudan or brought thereinto before the year 1783 of the Gregorian Calendar,

" Immovable
Antiquities."

"Immovable Antiquities" mean antiquities attached to the soil or only removed with difficulty therefrom and

" Movable
Antiquities."

"Movable Antiquities" mean all antiquities other than immovable antiquities.

" Conservator
of Antiquities."

"Conservator of Antiquities" shall include any person appointed to officiate for or to act as the deputy of the Conservator of Antiquities and also until a Conservator of Antiquities is appointed and during any vacancy in the appointment any person appointed by the Governor General to perform the duties of the Conservator of Antiquities under this Ordinance.

Power to
proclaim
buildings etc.
Antiquities.

(ii) The Governor General shall have power by notice published in the Sudan Gazette to constitute any building or other thing attached to the soil or only removable therefrom with difficulty which was built or made in or after the year 1783 an immovable antiquity within the meaning of this Ordinance.

Antiquities to
be property of
Government.

3. Every antiquity whether movable or immovable that now is or hereafter is found on or under the surface of the soil shall be the property of the Government and no such antiquity and no movable antiquity now in the hands of private persons shall be alienable without the consent of the Conservator of Antiquities and no person shall acquire by purchase or otherwise a good title to any such antiquity without such consent.

4. The Government shall have power to acquire under the Land Acquisition Ordinance 1903 or any similar Ordinance for the time being in force the site of any immovable antiquity which is not situated on Government lands and any necessary right of way or means of access thereto and also shall be entitled to render movable and to remove at any time from any lands not Government lands any immovable antiquity which has vested in the Government under the provisions of this Ordinance paying only for actual loss occasioned to the owner and occupier of the land. In valuing land for such acquisition no account shall be taken of the existence or value of antiquities which are existing or have been found on or in such land.

Power of Government to acquire Sites of antiquities.

1903 No. 1.

5. Any person who discovers an immovable antiquity and any owner or occupier of land where an immovable antiquity has been discovered who knows of such discovery and any Sheikh or Omda who knows of such discovery and does not report the same within a reasonable time to the Inspector or Mamur of his district shall be liable on conviction to imprisonment for a term not exceeding one month or to fine or to both. A reasonable time shall mean such time as seems reasonable to the magistrate trying the case in all the circumstances thereof.

Discovery of immovable antiquities to be reported.

6. Any person who wilfully injures or destroys any immovable antiquity without the consent of the Conservator of Antiquities or who without the consent of the Conservator of Antiquities takes possession of or removes any materials and thereby causes the injury or destruction of any immovable antiquity or who converts any immovable antiquity to any use which is likely to injure or destroy it or alter its character shall be liable on conviction to imprisonment for a term not exceeding one year or to fine or to both.

Punishment for injury to or destruction of immovable antiquities.

7. (i) Any person who finds a movable antiquity on or under the surface of the soil and does not report the finding or bring or send the article within a reasonable time as hereinbefore defined to the Inspector or Mamur of his district shall be liable on conviction to imprisonment not exceeding one month or to a fine or to both.

Discovery of movable antiquities to be reported.

(ii) Any person bringing or sending an article as aforesaid shall take a receipt from the person to whom he delivers it.

Receipt to be taken.

Election of purchase to Government of movable antiquities.

(iii) Where an article has been reported or brought as in the *first subsection of this* section mentioned the Conservator of Antiquities shall elect whether or not to take the article on behalf of the Government. If the Conservator of Antiquities elects to take the article he shall pay the finder if the article consists of gold silver or precious stones the intrinsic value of the article without reference to its workmanship or antiquity and if the article does not consist of gold silver or precious stones he shall pay the finder half the market value of the article. The market value of the article shall be fixed by the Conservator of Antiquities and his decision shall be final subject only to the right of the finder if he refuses the sum offered by the Conservator of Antiquities to appeal within three months to the Governor General.

When finder entitled.

(iv) If the Conservator of Antiquities elects not to take the article as aforesaid the finder shall be entitled to the article and to a statement of disclaimer from the Conservator of Antiquities and a license in writing to sell or otherwise deal with the said article. Such license shall be in such a form as shall be fixed from time to time by the Government.

§ 7. (iii) *The words in italics were substituted by the Revision Ordinance (No. 2) 1906 (1906 No.   ) for the original word.*

Excavations without permission forbidden.

8. Any person carrying on diggings excavations or clearings whether in his own land or in another person's for the purpose of looking for antiquities except under an authorization from the Conservator of Antiquities shall be liable on conviction to imprisonment for a term not exceeding one year or to a fine or to both. Such authorization shall be in writing and shall specify the place where and the time within which such diggings excavations or clearing may be carried on and may be made subject to any arrangement between the person to whom the permission is given and the Government as to the Government ceding its right of ownership in any articles found.

Sale of antiquities.

9. No person shall sell or offer for sale any antiquity unless he holds a license in writing of the Conservator of Antiquities to sell the same. On every sale the license shall be handed over to the purchaser and no such sale shall be valid unless such license is so handed over. Any person selling or offering for sale any antiquity without such license or without handing over such license to the purchaser and any person purchasing any antiquity without taking over such license shall be liable on conviction to imprisonment for a term not exceeding three months or to a fine or to both.

10. Any person exporting or attempting to export any antiquity without being in possession of the license for sale as aforesaid or of a special permission from the Conservator of Antiquities to export such antiquity shall be liable on conviction to imprisonment for a term not exceeding three months or to fine or to both.

Export of antiquities.

11. Any person found in possession of a movable antiquity which he is unable to show that he obtained lawfully and in good faith shall be liable on conviction to imprisonment for a term not exceeding three months or to fine or to both.

Possession of antiquity not obtained lawfully and in good faith to be punishable.

12. The Governor of a Province shall have power to forbid digging for sobakh in any place except under such restrictions as are thought fit and any person digging in any forbidden place shall be liable on conviction to a term of imprisonment not exceeding one month or to a fine or to both.

Sebakh digging may be prohibited.

13. Any antiquity the subject of an offence under this Ordinance may be confiscated to the Government by the Court trying the offence.

Confiscation of antiquities.

14. Where an offence under this Ordinance is also an offence under the Sudan Penal Code the offender may be proceeded against either under this Ordinance or under the said Code.

How offence may be tried.
1899 No 11.

15. Offences under this Ordinance may be tried by the court of a magistrate of the second class or any higher court and summarily or otherwise.

Jurisdiction.

16. In the trial of any offence under this Ordinance where there is any doubt whether an alleged antiquity was built produced or made before the year 1783 the production of the written opinion of the Conservator of Antiquities that such alleged antiquity was built produced or made before that date shall throw the burden of proof that it was not so on the person alleging the contrary and if it is asserted that any alleged antiquity was brought into the Sudan since the first January 1783 it shall rest with the person making such assertion to prove the same.

Burden of proof.

1905 No. 9.

THE DEMARCATION AND SURVEY OBDINANCE 1905.

Promulgated in Sudan Gazette No. 80 of 24 Aug. 1905.

An ordinance for facilitating the demarcation of boundaries and the making of surveys.

IT IS HEREBY ENACTED as follows :—

Short title.

1. This Ordinance may be called "The Demarcation and Survey Ordinance 1905."

Authority to demarcate or survey lands.

2. It shall be lawful for the Governor General and the Director General of Surveys and the Governor of a Province as regards land within his province and any other officer thereto empowered by Ordinance severally by an instrument in writing signed by him to authorize any officer of the Government to demarcate or survey any lands described in such instrument.

General powers of Survey Officer.

3. (i) Any officer authorized to demarcate or survey any lands may at any reasonable time enter upon any lands which he is required to demarcate or survey and upon lands contiguous thereto and may make any inquiries and may fix any stone post pillar or other boundary or survey mark in or upon the land and may dig up any ground for the purpose of fixing the same and may cut down and remove any timber or other growth which may obstruct any survey line; provided always that as little damage as possible shall be done to the land or to any property thereon.

(ii) The officer so demarcating or surveying the land shall forthwith assess the value of any damage done and shall pay or tender the amount so assessed to the owners thereof.

(iii) Any dispute regarding the sufficiency of the amount so paid or tendered shall be determined by the Governor General or an officer deputed by him.

(iv) Provided that no compensation shall be given to the owner or occupier of any land on account of damage reasonably done in the process of demarcating the boundaries of land owned or occupied by him.

4. Any officer authorized to demarcate or survey any land may order any person or persons occupying or otherwise interested in such land or any land abutting thereon or any person employed on or in connection with such land or any person who can give any information regarding the boundaries of such land or in whose possession or power any document relating to such boundaries is alleged to be

Power of Survey Officer to summon persons to give information.

(*a*) to attend before him at a fixed time and place,

(*b*) to point out the boundaries of the land,

(*c*) to give any information required for the purpose of the demarcation or survey,

(*d*) to produce any document in his power or possession relating to such boundaries.

Such order may be in the form contained in Schedule A.

5. (i) Any officer authorized to demarcate or survey any land may order the owner or occupier of such land within a reasonable time to be fixed by such officer

Owners and occupiers may be ordered to demarcate their lands.

(*a*) to demarcate his land and for the purpose of such demarcation to erect such stones pillars posts or other boundary or land marks as the said officer may direct,

(*b*) to clear any boundary or other line which it may be necessary to clear for the purpose of the demarcation of his land,

(*c*) to provide labour or otherwise assist in the demarcation of his land.

Such order may be in the form contained in Schedule B.

(ii) If the lands shall not be demarcated within the time and in the manner directed by the said officer the said officer may after due enquiry mark out the boundaries of the land and unless boundary marks of a suitable description have already been erected may cause the same to be erected and may clear any boundary or other lines which it may be convenient to clear for the purpose of such demarcation.

If order not obeyed Survey Officer may demarcate.

(iii) All costs incurred under the last subsection may be assessed by the said officer and upon application to a magistrate of the first or second class under the Sudan Civil Justice Ordinance 1900 may be recovered from the owner or occupier in the same manner as land tax in arrear.

Cost to be borne by owner or occupier.
1900 No, 2.

Liability of people to obey orders.

6. (i) Every person called upon to do any of the matters mentioned in the last two sections shall be legally bound so far as he may be able to do any of such things which he may be so called on to do.

Service of notices.

(ii) A notice calling upon any person to do any of the matters mentioned in the last two sections may be addressed to him individually or to him and other persons jointly and shall unless the contrary appears be deemed to have been communicated to him if delivered to the Sheikh of the village in which the land in question is situated

Land-marks to be maintained.

7. The owners and occupiers of any lands which have been officially demarcated shall be bound to keep and maintain the land boundary marks in good repair and to replace any which are destroyed or removed.

Land-marks may be placed in charge of one owner.

8. The Governor or an Inspector may at any time order in writing which of the adjoining owners shall be entrusted with the charge of any land-mark or boundary mark. Such order may be in the form contained in Schedule C.

Repair, etc., of land-marks.

9. Whenever a Governor Inspector or Mamur becomes aware that any land or boundary mark within the local limits of his jurisdiction is in bad repair or has been injured destroyed or removed he may cause the same to be repaired or replaced and may recover the cost from the person if any who is bound to maintain such mark.

Duties of Sheikhs as regards land-marks.

10. It shall be the duty of every sheikh of a village to prevent the injury destruction or removal of any official land mark boundary mark or survey mark within the local limits of his jurisdiction and to report immediately to the Mamur whenever he becomes aware that any such mark has been so interfered with.

Penalties for defacing, etc., land-marks.

11. Whoever defaces removes injures or otherwise impairs any land mark boundary mark or survey mark unless duly authorized to do so shall be liable upon conviction by a magistrate to imprisonment for a term which may extend to one year or to fine or to both.

SCHEDULE "A"
Notice to Attend and Furnish Information.

To the owners and occupiers of the (sagia) land numbered .... .. in the village of........... . . or to A B owner of   .   Take notice that by virtue of section 4 of the Demarcation and Survey Ordinance 1905 you are hereby required (either personally or by your authorized agent)

(a) to meet   at   .... on the ....day of .... and not to depart without his permission,

(b) to point out to him the boundaries of the land owned or occupied by you,

(c) to furnish him with any information which he may require for the purpose of the survey,

(d) to produce to him any document in your power or possession relating to the boundaries of such land.

SCHEDULE "B."
Notice to Assist in Demarcation.

To the owners and occupiers of the .... lands in the village of   .   _   or to A B of   .
Take notice that by virtue of the power given by section 5 of the Demarcation and Survey Ordinance 1905 you are hereby (respectively) required

(a) to fix or repair the boundary marks of the lands so owned or occupied by you before the . ..... day of............

(b) to clear the boundary lines of such lands,

(c) to meet the said ... .on the   day of .. ..   on the land so owned or occupied by you and to assist him in the demarcation of the said land.

SCHEDULE "C."
Notice to Maintain Boundary Marks.

To .. .   .
Take notice that by virtue of the powers given by section 8 of the Demarcation and Survey Ordinance 1905 I hereby order that the boundary and land marks erected on your land and specified on the back hereof are placed under your charge and you are hereby required to keep and maintain the same in good repair.

1905 No. 10.

THE OFFICIALS' SALARIES ORDINANCE 1905.

Promulgated in Sudan Gazette No. 82 of 1 October 1905.

An Ordinance for regulating the taking in execution of the salaries and pay of Government Officials.

IT IS HEREBY ENACTED as follows :—

Short title.

1. This Ordinance may be cited as "The Officials' Salaries Ordinance 1905."

Salaries of officials to be unassignable and not liable to execution.

2. Subject as hereinafter provided the pay salary allowances and other sums due to any Government official or employee in his capacity as such from the Government or any Department thereof cannot be assigned or charged by such official or employee and shall not be attached by any court or otherwise taken in execution whether at the time of such assignment charge attachment or execution any sums are then due and owing to such official or employee or not.

Exceptions as to Government debts and family allowances.

3. Notwithstanding section 2 hereof the pay salary allowances or other sums as aforesaid due to any Government official or employee may be set off against any debts incurred by such official or employee to the Government and a deduction of not more than one quarter of the total pay or salary may be made to pay maintenance alimony or other family allowances ordered to be paid by a court of competent authority.

Bankruptcy.

4. Notwithstanding section 2 hereof in the event of any Government official or employee being declared bankrupt the court or the person administering the bankrupt's estate shall receive for distribution among the creditors so much of the bankrupt's pay or salary as the court with the consent of the chief officer of the department under which the pay or salary is enjoyed may order. Before making any such order the court shall communicate with the chief officer of the department as to the amount time and manner of the payment to itself or to such person as aforesaid and shall obtain the written consent of the chief officer of the department to the terms of such payment.

1905 No. 11.
THE LAND TAX ORDINANCE 1905.
Promulgated in Sudan Gazette No. 82 of 1 October 1905.

An Ordinance for amending the Land Tax Ordinance 1899, and for the repeal of the Land Tax Ordinance 1901.

IT IS HEREBY ENACTED as follows : —

1. This Ordinance may be cited as " The Land Tax Ordinance 1905," and shall be construed as one with " The Land Tax Ordinance 1899." *Short title.* *1899 No 3.*

2. " The Land Tax Ordinance 1901" is hereby repealed and the whole of section 1 of " The Land Tax Ordinance 1899 " after the words " at the rates following that is to say" shall be and remain repealed. *Repeals.* *1901 No. 6.* *1899 No. 3.*

3. For that part of section 1 of " The Land Tax Ordinance 1899 " which is and remains repealed shall be substituted the following : — *Classification of lands.* *1899 No. 3.*

1st rate	...	...	P.T. 60 per feddan.
2nd rate	...	...	P.T. 50 per feddan.
3rd rate	...	...	P.T. 40 per feddan.
4th rate	...	...	P.T. 30 per feddan.
5th rate	...	...	P.T. 20 per feddan.
6th rate	...	...	P.T. 10 per feddan.

1905 No. 12.
THE CUSTOMS ORDINANCE 1905
Promulgated in Sudan Gazette No. 84 of 1 Dec. 1905.

An Ordinance reducing the customs duty on certain articles.

IT IS HEREBY ENACTED as follows :—

1. This Ordinance may be cited as "The Customs Ordinance 1905" and comes into force at once. *Short title and commencement.*

2. The import duty is reduced from 8 per cent ad valorem to 4 per cent ad valorem on the following articles : — *Import duties on certain articles reduced.*

(*a*) Coal, mazut, charcoal, and firewood,
(*b*) Timber,
(*c*) Petroleum,
(*d*) Oxen, cows, sheep, and goats and the meat of those animals.

Agreement for Administration of Sudan.

AGREEMENT between HER BRITANNIC MAJESTY'S GOVERN-
MENT and the GOVERNMENT of HIS HIGHNESS the KHEDIVE
of EGYPT relative to the future Administration of the
Sudan.

Published in Sudan Gazette No 1. of 7 March 1899.

WHEREAS certain provinces in the Sudan which were in
rebellion against the authority of His Highness the Khedive have
now been reconquered by the joint military and financial efforts
of Her Britannic Majesty's Government and the Government of
His Highness the Khedive;

AND whereas it has become necessary to decide upon a system
for the administration of and for the making of laws for the said
reconquered provinces, under which due allowance may be made
for the backward and unsettled condition of large portions thereof,
and for the varying requirements of different localities;

AND whereas it is desired to give effect to the claims which
have accrued to Her Britannic Majesty's Government by right of
conquest, to share in the present settlement and future working
and development of the said system of administration and legislation;

AND whereas it is conceived that for many purposes Wadi
Halfa and Suakin may be most effectively administered in conjunction with the reconquered provinces to which they are respectively adjacent;

NOW it is hereby agreed and declared by and between the
undersigned, duly authorized for that purpose, as follows:—

ART. I.

The word "Sudan" in this agreement means all the territories
South of the 22nd parallel of latitude, which:

(1). Have never been evacuated by Egyptian troops since the
year 1882: or

(2). Which having before the late rebellion in the Sudan been
administered by the Government of His Highness the Khedive
were temporarily lost to Egypt and have been reconquered by

Her Majesty's Government and the Egyptian Government, acting in concert: or

(3). Which may hereafter be reconquered by the two Governments acting in concert.

ART. II.

The British and Egyptian flags shall be used together both on land and water, throughout the Sudan, except in the town of Suakin, in which locality the Egyptian flag alone shall be used.

ART. III.

The supreme military and civil command in the Sudan shall be vested in one officer, termed the "Governor-General of the Sudan". He shall be appointed by Khedivial Decree on the recommendation of Her Britannic Majesty's Government, and shall be removed only by Khedivial Decree, with the consent of Her Britannic Majesty's Government.

ART. IV.

Laws, as also Orders and Regulations with the full force of law, for the good government of the Sudan, and for regulating the holding disposal and devolution of property of every kind therein situate may from time to time be made altered or abrogated by Proclamation of the Governor General. Such Laws Orders and Regulations may apply to the whole or any named part of the Sudan, and may, either explicitly or by necessary implication, alter or abrogate any existing Law or Regulation.

All such Proclamations shall be forthwith notified to Her Britannic Majesty's Agent and Consul General in Cairo, and to the President of the Council of Ministers of His Highness the Khedive.

ART. V.

No Egyptian Law Decree Ministerial Arrêté, or other enactment hereafter to be made or promulgated shall apply to the Sudan or any part thereof, save in so far as the same shall be applied by Proclamation of the Governor General in manner hereinafter provided.

Art. VI.

In the definition by Proclamation of the conditions under which Europeans, of whatever nationality, shall be at liberty to trade with or reside in the Sudan, or to hold property within its limits, no special privileges shall be accorded to the subjects of any one or more Power.

Art. VII.

Import duties on entering the Sudan shall not be payable on .goods coming from Egyptian territory. Such duties may however be levied on goods coming from elsewhere than Egyptian territory, but in the case of goods entering the Sudan at Suakin or any other port on the Red Sea Littoral, they shall not exceed the corresponding duties for the 'time being leviable on goods entering Egypt from abroad. Duties may be levied on goods leaving the Sudan, at such rates as may from time to time be prescribed by Proclamation.

Art. VIII.

The Jurisdiction of the Mixed Tribunals shall not extend, nor be recognized for any purpose whatsoever, in any part of the Sudan, except in the town of Suakin.

Art. IX.

Until, and save so far as it shall be otherwise determined by proclamation, the Sudan, with the exception of the town of Suakin, shall be and remain under martial law.

Art. X.

No Consuls, Vice-Consuls, or Consular Agents shall be accredited in respect of nor allowed to reside in the Sudan, without the previous consent of Her Britannic Majesty's Government.

Art. XI.

The importation of slaves into the Sudan, as also their exportation, is absolutely prohibited. Provision shall be made by Proclamation for the enforcement of this Regulation.

Art. XII.

It is agreed between the two Governments that special attention shall be paid to the enforcement of the Brussels Act of the 2nd July, 1890, in respect of the import, sale, and manufacture of fire-arms and their munitions, and distilled or spirituous liquors.

Done in Cairo, the 19th January, 1899.

Signed { Boutros Ghali.
Cromer.

AGREEMENT made between the BRITISH and EGYPTIAN GOVERN-
MENTS Supplemental to the Agreement made between the two
Governments on 19th January 1899 for the future adminis-
tration of the Sudan.

Published in Sudan Gazette No. 50 of 1 August 1903.

WHEREAS under our Agreement made the 19th day of January
1899, relative to the future administration of the Sudan, it is
provided by Article VIII, that the jurisdiction of the Mixed
Tribunals shall not extend nor be recognized for any purpose
whatsoever in any part of the Sudan except in the town of
Suakin :

AND WHEREAS no Mixed Tribunal has ever been established at
Suakin and it has been found to be inexpedient to establish
any such tribunal in that locality by reason notably of the
expense which the adoption of this measure would occasion :

AND WHEREAS grievous injustice is caused to the inhabitants
of Suakin by the absence of any local jurisdiction for the settlement of their disputes and it is expedient that the town of Suakin
should be placed upon the same footing as the rest of the Sudan :

AND WHEREAS we have decided to modify our said Agreement accordingly in manner hereinafter appearing :—

Now, it is hereby agreed and declared by and between the
Undersigned duly authorized for that purpose, as follows :—

ARTICLE I.

Those provisions of our agreement of the 19th day of January
1899 by which the town of Suakin was excepted from the general
regime established by the said Agreement for the future administration of the Sudan, are hereby abrogated.

Done at Cairo, the 10th of July, 1899. .

Signed { BOUTROS GHALI,
           CROMER.

ARRANGEMENT made between the EGYPTIAN and the SUDAN GOVERN-MENT as to Reciprocal Service of Process and Surrender of or Execution of Sentences against Fugitive Offenders.

Published in Sudan Gazette No. 37 of July 1902.

I. *Service of Process.*

1. Each Government undertakes, in principle, the service and notification of summonses and other legal documents forwarded by the other Government.

2. Every document forwarded for service shall, so far as practicable, be sent in duplicate, and shall be accompanied by such information as may be in the possession of the forwarding Government as to the whereabouts of the person on whom the document is to be served.

3. Documents forwarded for service in the Sudan shall be sent through the Ministry of Justice to the Sudan Agent, Cairo, who will arrange for their service in manner prescribed by the Governor General.

4. Documents forwarded for service in Egypt shall be sent through the Sudan Agent to the Ministry of Justice, which will arrange for their service administratively.

5. The Government charged with the service of any document shall, so soon as may be after service has been effected forward, to the other Government, through the channels above prescribed a certificate of service, duly authenticated, indicating the place, time and method of service. If the document has been sent in duplicate, one copy shall be returned with the certificate.

Whenever it is found impossible to effect service information to that effect shall be forwarded through the same channels.

II. *Surrender of Fugitive Offenders.*

6. Each Government undertakes, in principle the surrender, on the demand of the other Government, of

(*a*) persons whom there is reason to believe to be guilty of any offence triable by the Courts of the Government making the demand and punishable with imprisonment for six months or more, or with any heavier penalty, and against whom a warrant of arrest has been issued in respect of such offence :

(*b*) persons who, being confined in the prisons of the Government making the demand, in execution of a legal sentence, have escaped and taken refuge in the other country.

7. The Sudan Government will further surrender on the demand of the Egyptian Government, but subject to the conditions hereinafter contained, persons sentenced to imprisonment for six months or upwards or to any heavier penalty by judgments of the Egyptian Courts satisfying the conditions required by Article 11 of the present arrangement.

8. The demand of surrender when made by the Egyptian Government shall ordinarily be made by the Ministry of Justice, and forwarded to the Sudan Agent, Cairo, who will arrange for the execution of such demand in manner prescribed by the Governor General.

9. Demands made by the Sudan Government shall be passed through the Sudan Agent, Cairo, to the Ministry of Justice, which will arrange for their execution in concert with the Ministry of the Interior.

10. Demands of surrender shall not, in principle, be made in respect of persons who are in Egypt, entitled to the benefit of the capitulations. Nevertheless the Egyptian Government may either demand or accord the surrender of any such person after first securing the assent of the consular authority interested. But the Sudan Government shall not be entitled to call on the Egyptian Government to apply for such assent.

11. Demands of surrender in virtue of an Egyptian judgment shall be made only

(*a*) when the judgment purports to have been pronounced in the presence of the accused or to be a judgment "per contumace" (*i.e.* to have been pronounced in the absence of the accused, on a charge of crime) or

(*b*) where the judgment purports to be "by default" (*i.e.* to have been pronounced on a charge of misdemeanour, in the absence of the accused), when it is established that the accused appeared once at least before the Court or before the enquiring magistrate, or that while in Egypt he had notice of the proceedings against him either by personal service upon him of a summons to appear or otherwise, or that the judgment has been personally served upon him in time to allow him to make opposition thereto or to appeal against it.

12. The demand of surrender shall in every case be accompanied by such information as is available as to the identity and whereabouts of the person whose surrender is demanded.

13. It shall further be accompanied by the following evidence and documents:

(a) When the demand is made in virtue of a warrant of arrest:— by the warrant of arrest or a certified copy thereof, and a certified copy of the police procès-verbal and the depositions already made before the enquiring magistrate, if the demand is made by the Egyptian Government, or of the proceedings already taken before the committing magistrate if the demand is made by the Sudan Government:

(b) When the demand is for the surrender of an escaped person:—by a certified copy of the authority under which the offender was confined, and by duly authenticated evidence of the escape of the offender.

(c) When the demand is made in virtue of an Egyptian judgment:—by a certified copy of the judgment or of the warrant of execution based thereon, by a certificate from the Ministry of Justice that the judgment has become executory, and, in the case of a judgment by default, by duly authenticated evidence showing that the conditions required by Article 11 are satisfied.

14. Each Government shall prescribe, by rules, the procedure to be followed in the case of demands of surrender addressed to it. Such rules shall provide for the arrest of the person named in the demand and for his examination as to his identity and generally as to the case, and shall prescribe the authority by which it is to be decided whether a case for surrender has been made out in accordance with the terms of the present arrangement.

15. It shall in every case be open to the accused person to establish before the authority by whom the examination is conducted that he was not in the country of the Government by which his surrender is demanded at the date of the offence with which he is charged, in cases where the demand is based on a warrant of arrest or a judgement delivered in his absence, or at the date of the judgment which is alleged to have been delivered in his presence, or at the date of his alleged escape from prison, as the case may be.

16. Whenever a demand is made for the surrender of a person with a view to his trial, and the Courts of the country to which the demand is addressed are competent to try the offence with which he is charged, such Government may order that he be put upon his trial before its own Courts instead of granting his surrender.

17. When it is impossible at the date of making the demand to furnish at once the documents and evidence required by the present arrangement the person whose surrender is demanded may, in the discretion of the Government to which the demand is addressed, be provisionally arrested pending the arrival of the necessary documents and evidence, which shall be forwarded at the earliest possible moment.

18. Mudirs in either country shall have power to provisionally arrest persons found within their jurisdiction, upon receiving credible information that such persons are fugitives from the other country and that they have there escaped from prison, or that a warrant of arrest has been or is about to be issued there against them. In every case of arrest in virtue of the provisions of the present article the Mudir shall immediately report to his own Government.

19. Whenever a Mudir has reason to believe that a person whose surrender may be demanded under the present arrangement is flying from his jurisdiction to the other country, he may send information thereof direct to the Mudir of the District in the other country to which such fugitive is believed to be proceeding, and the Mudir receiving such information may take action thereon conformably to the provisions of the last preceding article.

Each Mudir shall in such cases report his action immediately to his own Government.

III. *Execution of Egyptian Sentences in the Sudan.*

20. The Sudan Government will, at the request of the Egyptian Government, itself execute in the Sudan sentences of imprisonment for less than six months passed by Egyptian judgments in all cases in which if the sentence had exceeded six months the Egyptian Government would under the provisions of Part II of this arrangement have been entitled to the surrender of the offender in virtue of the judgment. The procedure in such cases shall, as nearly as may be, be the same as that under Part II of this arrangement.

IV. *Miscellaneous.*

21. Each Government shall pay to the other, on demand, all expenses actually incurred in execution of a demand of surrender addressed to such other Government or in serving documents sent for service to such other Government. The Egyptian Government will also pay to the Sudan Government on demand the costs of and incidental to the execution of sentences by the Sudan Government under the provisions of Article 20.

22. Where documents are sent for service on behalf of private persons, the Government to which they are sent may require, as a condition of such service, the payment of reasonable fees in additon to out of pocket expenses.

23. The Sudan Government will, as soon as may be, put into force such legislation as may be necessary for giving effect to the present arrangement.

24. The present arrangement shall not be construed as derogating from the provisions of Article 6 (2) of the Egyptian Judgments Ordinance, 1901.

25. The word "Mudir" in the present arrangement shall include "Governor" and "Administrator".

Approved by His Excellency the Governor General of the Sudan at Khartoum on the 8th May, 1902, and by the Council of Ministers of His Highness The Khedive at their meeting of the 17th May, 1902.

Order for Reciprocal Service Summons and Judgments
in Egypt and Sudan.

In connection with the above arrangement the following order was issued as No. 222 of the Sudan Government Orders 1904.

Sudan Courts: Method of Serving Summonses in Egypt.

Summonses of the Sudan Courts which it is desired to serve in Egypt should in future be sent direct by Governors of Provinces or Civil Judges or the Kadis of Mohammedan Law Courts to the Agent General, and will be returned in the same way.

Similarly, summonses of Egyptian Courts which it is desired to serve in the Sudan will be sent direct from the Agent General to Governors of Provinces, and returned in the same way.

Judgments of the Sudan Mohammedan Law Courts, however, which it is desired to have executed in Egypt, should be sent through the High Mohammedan Law Court and the Legal Secretary's Office: and in like manner judgments of the Egyptian Mohammedan Law Courts which it is desired to execute in the Sudan will be sent by the Agent General to the Legal Secretary.

INDEX.

INDEX.

The Ordinances the Titles of which are printed in Italics have been repealed.

Crops.

Cruelty to Animals.

Customs Duties.

Date Tax ... ... 16.

Date Trees.

Demarcation of Lands ... ... 160.

Dongola Town Lands ... ... 1, 44.

Donkeys.

Drunkenness.

Dueim Town Lands ... ... 105.

Duty.

Egyptian Judgment. ... ...45, 47, 107, 171, 175, 176.

Egyptian Legislation ... ... 167.

Pension—*continued.*

1/7/1C